J. PARKINSON
AUGUST 1984

J. PARKINSON
124 LONDON ROAD
LONG SUTTON
LINCS.
PE12 9EE
TEL: 0406 362388

J. PARKINSON
AUGUST 1984

L.M.S. MISCELLANY

A Pictorial Record of the Company's Activities in the Public Eye and Behind the Scenes

Volume Two

H. N. Twells

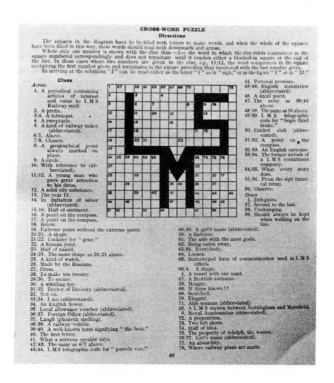

Oxford Publishing Company

ISBN 0-86093-290-7

Typesetting by:
Aquarius Typesetting Services, New Milton, Hants.

Printed in Great Britain by:
Netherwood Dalton & Co. Ltd., Huddersfield, Yorks.

ACKNOWLEDGEMENTS

Many of the friends who supplied photographs and information from their own collections for the first volume of *LMS Miscellany* have kindly done so again.

My thanks in particular are due to Roy Anderson, Robin Barr, Noel Coates, Gordon Coltas, John Edgington, John Miller, Barry Lane, Don Rowland, Bill Stubbs, David Tee and Graham Warburton, all devotees of the LMS and fellow members of The LMS Society. Glen Foxley wrote, following the publication of the first volume, to offer official material he had collected, though the ticket issues shown are mostly from the collection of Glyn Waite, also a member of the Society. Barry Hilton kindly loaned his collection of original postcards, and it is a great pity that these cannot be reproduced in colour. Other friends also helped immensely, and to each and every one I offer my sincere thanks.

One is always on the lookout for fresh sources of information on the railway scene prior to nationalization, and during a visit to 'Railwayana' in Sheffield the owner, Brian Hinchliffe, responded to my enquiry for photographs of the Ljungstrom turbine engine by offering the loan of his university degree thesis on steam turbine locomotives, and again I record my thanks and appreciation for this generous gesture.

Photographs from the National Collection are reproduced by kind permission of the Keeper of the National Railway Museum, and are Crown Copyright.

During the preparation of this volume, I was saddened to learn of the death of A. G. Ellis - George Ellis, a friend for many years, who even when so very ill a few months earlier, had welcomed me into his home to talk railways and to look through more of his print collection. George did so much to record the railway scene, particularly the LMS, and his name will always be remembered for his excellent work.

Proof reading and checking the manuscript has been undertaken by Chris Crofts and whilst doing so, he also set about the task of identifying as many freight vehicles as he could. Again, my sincere thanks.

LMS Miscellany - (Volume One) - amendments and additional information

Plates 3 & 4 are transposed to the captions
Plates 75 & 76 are transposed to the captions
The company title was: The London Midland & Scottish Railway Company and the word 'Limited' did not form part of it. The railway companies were set up following the Railways Act 1921, and although they were required to conform to company law in the production of accounts, and could issue capital stock for subscription by the public, the title did not include the word 'Limited', so apologies are offered for this error.
Plate 99 I am indebted to Keith King for some additional information relating to this photograph. His father served on the Birmingham Canal Navigation Co., and he has identified the boat to the left of the basin as *Horace*, the only LMS boat equipped with a Thornycroft engine and flexible drive coupled to the propeller, which could be raised or lowered as required to suit the load and depth of water. In the Birmingham area, the LMS owned 125 canal boats. The Company were major shareholders in the BCN, and had representative Directors on the Board, with a railway 'Chairman' having a casting vote role.

British Library Cataloguing in Publication Data

Twells, H. N.
  LMS miscellany.
  1. London, Midland and Scottish Railway
  —History—Pictorial works   2. Railroads
  —Great Britain—Rolling-stock—History
  —Pictorial works
  I. Title
  625.2'0941   TF64.L8

Published by:
Oxford Publishing Co.
Link House
West Street
POOLE, Dorset

CONTENTS

INTRODUCTION

Memories of the LMS Railway live on in the minds of those who knew the Company as travellers or employees, and it is now more than 35 years since it ceased to exist as an independent organization. It follows therefore that one must be at least forty years of age to have been around and been able to take in much of the railway scene, and even then, five is a young and tender age! People below forty must therefore rely on photographic evidence for their insight into the LMS. The first volume of *LMS Miscellany* offers a selection of photographs which, for the most part, have not been published in other books and cover a range of subjects, many of which were not known to the traveller of the time. Such was the size and complexity of the Company's operations that one volume of around 250 photographs could in no way do justice to this vast empire. A further selection of photographs is offered in this second volume, but in no way do these complete the story. There is further material and subject matter available which is deeply interesting, and one problem is always present which poses the question as to what should be included.

My own memories of the LMS are from the late war years, and whilst my entire interest at that time was in the engines, I do recall changing at some of the large stations, Derby and Crewe in particular, and being fascinated by everything around me. Stations were so much busier, both with trains and passengers, and the moments before the arrival of an express were captivating, certainly for me. I well recall my grandma's advice of 'Don't stand near the edge when the train comes in', being totally ignored as the huge machines pulled alongside the platform. It was not until Don Rowland offered the picture of a Collecting Dog at Crewe that this feature of the railway scene was remembered - a ha'penny or penny was popped in the slot and the dog was dutifully stroked. My mother has since corrected one important milestone, in that my first journey by LMS train from Swadlincote to Coalville was not at twelve months but at less than two months old, and this in the late summer of 1937.

Over the years, my interest in engines and the running scene has given way to virtually everything but these aspects, and this is, of course, where most of the unpublished material of the LM&SR lies. There are several books dealing with rolling stock, engine sheds, branch lines and architecture, and a fascinating series of magazine articles by Don Rowland, which explained to the model railway fraternity that the LMS was not all red engines and red carriages. It was much more than this, and

he quoted the ratios of red engines to black engines, carriages and wagons in statistical terms. But no one, so far as I know, has given statistics or ratios for wagon stock to freight carried, nor even the figures to show the average number of times an LMS passenger seat was occupied. To satisfy the interest and curiosity of the few who would like this information the figures, as at 31st December 1935, are as follows:

Total number of wagon stock(brake vans not included: 5,593)	265,653
Total tonnage capacity	3,023,454 tons
Average tonnage capacity wagon stock	11,381 tons
Goods train traffic tonnage carried -	125,828,716 tons
plus livestock equated tonnage	971,036 tons
	126,799,752

Each wagon carried an average of 477 tons in 1935, and the average wagon carried a capacity load 42 times. This was less than once each week, but wagon stock seldom achieved a speedy turn-round.

Total goods train traffic receipts were		£35,917,652
- and each wagon averaged earnings of	£135 4s 0d	
- and each ton carried averaged earnings of	7s 4d	

Passenger traffic

The total number of seats in each class was	1st	127,514
	2nd	1,788
	3rd	925,448

The average number of passenger bottoms per carriage seat in 1935 was	1st	122
	2nd	127
	3rd	461

- and the overall average number of passenger bottoms per carriage seat for 1935 was		420
Passenger receipts amounted to		£19,575,627
- and each passenger seat earned an average £18 11s 5d in 1935.		

These statistics in isolation mean very little to most people, but they do serve to illustrate the detailed records which the Company required its employees to maintain for its purposes, and also to enable it to submit figures in standardized form, along with the other railway companies, to the Ministry of Transport. Vast quantities of paper moved about the system, and we must remember that there were no computers and on-line terminals, the figures being collated by hand and only in the central audit offices did the Company provide the simplest of adding machines. Pen-pushing was a major occupation, and most of it was repetitively boring day in and day out.

The search through statistical records, old files and official publications prepared by, or on behalf of the Company, continues to fascinate me, and as fresh photographic material comes to hand, I hope that more of this will be made available for a wider audience and future generations.

A number of ticket issues were illustrated in the first volume, but the variety and type of ticket issued at one time or another by the Company can only be quantified by saying it was enormous. Whilst not wishing to include just one plate of tickets in this volume, I did think it appropriate to include a further selection of ticket issues. So I have, therefore, selected those which are appropriate either to the section text or to the station illustrated, in the hope that these will add further interest for the reader.

Finally, I have been greatly encouraged by comments received after the publication of the first volume of *LMS Miscellany*, and it is pleasing to know that my original aim of providing a selection of photographs of LMS activities the public did not normally see, or had perhaps forgotten through the passage of time, may well have been fulfilled. One comment received concluded 'I've really enjoyed it, I couldn't leave it, and I've got a Nottingham driver coming to see me later today - I'll shove it under his nose too!' My sincere thanks to those who wrote to me, and I hope this volume adds to the LM&SR story.

H. N. Twells
Chesterfield
1984

The LMS Employees

The London, Midland & Scottish Railway Co. was formed through the grouping of railways under the Railways Act 1921, and the Company was formed and operational from 1st January, 1923. Details of the formation and the various companies which were grouped to form the LM&SR are shown in the first volume of *LMS Miscellany*, along with details of the Company's interests in jointly operated lines and some of its railway related investments. Whilst the LM&SR could be identified, very little thought is ever given to the multiplicity of skilled and trained people who were employed to make the Company's assets a part of the service industry. Without them, the LM&SR would have been nothing.

Most material which has been published about the employees has been confined to the small number of officials who held specific office, and to those who gave distinguished service and were honoured by the Company. But what were the various grades of the workforce, and how many were in each grade in each of the principal departments? This was the workforce which made the LM&SR the force it was between the years 1923 and 1948, and the figures at 31st December 1935 are as follows:

LMS CENSUS OF STAFF - TOTAL NUMBER EMPLOYED

Male	- adults	199,416	
	juniors, apprentices, etc.	13,007	212,423
Female	adults	8,904	
	juniors	893	9,797
		Total	222,220

NUMBER OF EMPLOYEES IN PRINCIPAL GRADES CENSUS - ONE WEEK

Officers, clerical and technical staff

Officers & male clerical staff	25,018	
Women clerical staff	4,507	
Station masters, goods agents, etc.	2,000	
Technical staff	1,156	
Traffic control staff	878	33,559
Supervisory staff-all departments (other than shop and artizan, and police)		4,039

Conciliation staff

Locomotive department

Engine drivers	12,672	
Engine firemen	12,063	
Engine cleaners	3,365	
Shed staff and other grades	5,561	33,661

Traffic department

Foremen (other than supervisory)	1,690	
Guards - goods	5,875	
Guards - passenger	2,044	
Porters - all grades	9,441	
Shunters	6,163	
Signalmen	10,120	
Ticket collectors	1,020	
Parcels vanmen and boys	1,789	
Other grades	2,201	40,343

Goods department

Foremen - working	391	
Checkers, loaders, porters etc.	11,028	
Capstanmen	758	
Carters and vanguards	6,454	
Motor drivers and attendants	2,355	
Other grades	3,518	24,504

Carriage and wagon department

Carriage cleaners and washers		
- Male 2,675		
- Female 72	2,747	
Carriage & wagon examiners, oilers etc.	2,088	
Other grades	386	5,221

Civil engineer's deparment

Permanent way men	19,673	
Signal and telegraph staff	2,668	22,341

Total Conciliation Staff 126,070

Police staff including supervisory		732
Shop and artizan staff (other then clerical and technical and marine department)		
Supervisory - all departments	869	
Male staff		
Locomotive, carriage and wagon departments	29,995	
Civil engineer's department		
Permanent way	7,516	
Signal and telegraph	932	
Electrical engineer's department	792	
Electrical generating stations	425	
General stores, stationery & sheeting department	1,324	
Other departments	742	
Female Staff		
All departments	551	43,146
Ancilliary business staff (excluding clerical, except for the hotels)		
Canals	754	
Docks and quays	2,568	
Marine staff afloat - Male 1,548		
Female 40	1,588	
Motor omnibuses and road vehicles	5	
Hotel, refreshment rooms and dining cars (including clerical) Male 4,267		
Female 2,770	7,037	

Marine shop and artizan staff	309	12,261
Miscellaneous grades not allocated		
- Male 556		
- Female 1,857		2,413

Grand Total of LMS Employees 222,220

Artizan staff would embrace professionally qualified personnel, highly skilled specialists and managers of departments.

These figures are but a summary, which they have to be in a volume of this nature, but behind these figures, the LMS could rely on a dedicated and loyal workforce, perhaps at times more loyal than the Company could have expected.

Off duty, the employees engaged in a wide variety of activities, which were organized for their benefit and enjoyment. The use of Company premises for clubs and societies was common, which invariably led to the initials 'LMS' forming part of their title including the LMS Rifle Club, LMS Fur & Feather Society, LMS Ambulance Group and the LMS (London) Variety Orchestra, to name but a few. Competitions were organized between similarly interested groups around the system, and representative teams drawn from clubs and societies competed against the other railway company teams in national railway championships. There was no television, and radio programmes were, of necessity, formal and predictable so railway employees took their leisure time alongside some of the colleagues they worked with. The following photographs are of LMS employees.

Plate 1   LMS employees, forming the Rhyl LMS Male Voice Choir, with the trophy they won at the Rugby Musical Festival in 1932.
Pickering Collection

Plate 3   Mr A. Turley, who was Goods Inspector at Salford in 1937, smartly attired for this portrait which was probably taken when he received his new appointment.

B. Turley

Plate 2   What is believed to be the same group of employees as in the previous plate, posed in front of an ex-L&NWR carriage.
Pickering Collection

Plate 4   A small selection of cap badges.

G. Foxley Collection

Collecting Dogs

Charitable causes were never far from the hearts of railwaymen or passengers, and on the Western Division an old tradition, said to have dated from the L&NWR days, was continued by LMS staff. Collecting Dogs were paraded at the principal stations by retired railwaymen, and when passengers put coppers in the money box which was strapped to the dog's back, the dog either shook its money box, barked its appreciation, or both. Legend has it that the dogs were always black and at Crewe at least, they were always called *Prince*. The Company provided an allowance for the dog, and a uniform and wage to the handler.

This picture was taken on platform 1 of Crewe Station, looking north towards what was then No. 7 bay, and is believed to be in the late 1940s. Proceeds from the Crewe dogs went to the Webb Orphanage, an institution originated by the L&NWR in Crewe.

A special event in the life of one Collecting Dog was on 9th January 1933, when the President of the LMS, Sir Josiah Stamp, later Lord Stamp, presented an eleven year old collie dog called *Grace* and its owner, Ticket Collector Beer, with a gold medal. This was in recognition of having collected more than £200 from passengers at Dalston Junction Station, on the North London line out of Broad Street. The proceeds were sent to the Derby Railway Orphanage.

There were many other dogs with similar achievements which were recognized by the Company, but the real contribution of these dogs and their handlers was reflected in these orphanages being able to continue to care and give a home life to the many children who were less fortunate than the majority.

Plate 5 A 'Prince' in every sense of the word!

D. P. Rowland

Station Car Parking

Plate 6 An enamel black on yellow station car-park sign. In 1931, the LMS recognized that passengers may require to park motor cars close to the station from whence their rail journey commenced, and from January, areas were made available. By July, parking areas had been designated at more than 200 passenger stations and over 400 goods depots, and this was another useful source of revenue. At most locations, cars were charged at 1s per day, whilst motor cycles or three-wheeled vehicles were 6d per day, and in rural areas where demand was not so great, half these charges applied, although these were later brought into line. Cars could also accompany passengers, and station staff were encouraged to bring this service to the attention of car owners, where special rates were accorded to those purchasing first class tickets.

Author's Collection

Audit Office

Plate 7 A canvas bag, for use between Whatstandwell Station on the Derby to Manchester line and the audit office in Derby. Similar bags were used at all stations for fowarding the monthly statistical returns collated at each station, and the tickets collected from passengers which were required for audit verification purposes. The audit office had three main functions. These were a regular check on the recorded traffic receipts from each station, the calculation of traffic receipts applicable to through operations with other railway companies, and the compiling of statistical data. In addition, travelling auditors were employed to visit stations to verify the station accounting records, often arriving unannounced. They also undertook investigations of any matters brought to light through the audit procedures. Through traffic with the LNER and GWR companies was heavy, and a system of pooling receipts in relation to the traffic carried between each company was in operation, with the various pools shared equally. Statistical data was also required for submission to the Ministry of Transport, and to satisfy the accounting requirements of the various departments of the Company. One of the sidelines of the audit section was a fully-equipped ticket printing plant, attached to the Company's offices in London. The printing shop could produce 1,000,000 tickets from 1 ton of pasteboard, and the weekly capacity was 3½ tons of board. The used passenger tickets were sold after audit formalities were completed, for re-pulping into ticket board and similar requirements.

Author's Collection

Through Carriage Workings

'Through Express Services are in operation between the principal towns in England, Scotland and Wales, but through carriages are also run between places not directly connected by through express trains.' This announcement headed a table in the 1935 public timetable, but through carriages had long been a feature of the railways prior to this date, and continued thereafter.

What it meant was that one or possibly more carriages in the train would be detached at an intermediate station on the journey, and to save the long-distance passengers leaving the comfort of the specially designated carriage, it was shunted and attached to another train to continue its journey. Crewe was a major interchange, and it was a daily occurrence for Great Western chocolate and cream carriages to be shunted up to the relief express engine which was waiting at Crewe, then move with the engine on to the front of the express arrival from Euston, before proceeding to Glasgow. Similarly, LMS carriages worked through to Plymouth and Penzance with Great Western trains. Most through carriage workings were on Saturdays, with the majority running during the main holiday season, and it was then not uncommon to see complete trains of 'foreign carriages' working certain lines, particularly LMS stock to Paignton, Brighton and other locations. The vast majority of through workings were, however, LMS carriages merely changing trains to give a through service to points on the LMS system. One particularly interesting working must have been the 5.30p.m. ex-Glasgow Central train, with a through carriage for Penzance and a Pullman restaurant car from Glasgow to Carlisle, the only advertised Pullman working to Carlisle in 1925.

Plate 8 No. 6202, pictured at Shrewsbury, with a Great Western through carriage attached. It is interesting to see the man standing on the carriage roof, with a water pipe used to refill the toilet water tank, an operation not often recorded on film. Two wheel water tanks with hand pumps were used for this purpose.

A. G. Ellis

Plate 9 Hughes 4-6-0 No. 10461 and Compound No. 904, at the head of a Glasgow bound express in 1927, with the GWR through carriage from Plymouth to Glasgow having been attached at Crewe.

W. L. Good per W. T. Stubbs

Staff Accommodation and Amenities

Standards in accommodation were generally poor by today's minimum requirements under such Acts of Parliament as the Office, Shops & Railway Premises Acts, but when compared with much of industry, the railway-owned premises were quite good, and the companies did make efforts to raise the standards of the accommodation which they made available for employees to carry out their work. Nevertheless, lighting of premises was one aspect of the railway which was poor for much of the time, even when electricity replaced gas mantles.

It is understood that when the Midland Railway were building stations and offices in some locations, they entered into 99 year supply contracts with the local gas producing companies, and it was not until these ran out, or were bought out, that a change from gas to electricity was made.

Offices were somewhat austere, with linoleum on the floor, dark high desks and plain walls, to say nothing of the coal or coke fires which were becoming homely at the wrong end of the day. During the coldest periods of winter, overcoats were the norm for many employees, particularly those in goods and station offices.

In June 1936, the Labour and Establishment Office at Euston formulated a set of standards which, for all new works, were to be the minimum provided by the Company. Mr G. L. Darbyshire, Chief Officer for the L&E office in presenting the set of standards, also made it clear that where possible, existing accommodation should be brought up to these new minima, although it was recognized that the older establishments could not be altered structurally. Amenities generally were the 'fixtures and fittings', and these were improved.

The Standards for Staff Accommodation and Amenities were drawn to cover the following:

Office accommodation
Workmen's lavatories
Messrooms for wages staff
Bicycle storage
Drinking water at isolated locations
Wages staff hostels
Shunters' huts and traffic yards
Platelayers' Cabins

and within each section, a detailed specification was given. For general office accommodation, everything from the LMS standard unit wooden desk and the positioning of it, (at right angles to windows, and for preference, with the window to the left of staff when seated) to the provision of one wall calendar for each general room, was covered. The specification included several innovations to ensure ease of maintenance, including all electrical wiring for telephones, electric bells, lighting and machines, to be concentrated in ducts provided within walls or under floor levels, telephone and desk lighting requirements to be pre-planned, window areas to be not less than one-tenth of the floor area, and artificial lighting to be of general rather than individual lighting points whenever possible.

The general internal decorations included plain walls except for noticeboards positioned to suit individual operational requirements. Decorations were to the following specification:

Ceiling and frieze	White	
Walls	Cream	LMS
Dado	Green with 1in. deep black band at the top	standard shades

This colour scheme was also applied to older establishments, when they were redecorated. Toilet and locker accommodation was provided proportional to the number of male and female employees at the particular location. Where 'more than a few' females were employed, a specially equipped ambulance room was located in the female convenience area. Sorting and despatch letter rooms were provided where the volume of mail demanded such facilities and similarly, bookrooms and filing accommodation had to be sufficient for the types of work undertaken.

Motor cars were few and far between, and the vast majority of the population had nothing more than a bicycle as a means of transport. Many thousands used public transport, including local buses and trains to get to work, but those who cycled required bicycle storage when they arrived at the workplace, this being provided by countless lines of steel racks close by on railway property. Later, as the use of concrete became cheaper and more widespread, concrete blocks to take one wheel were provided, beneath concrete or corrugated iron shelters.

Wages staff hostels, better known as company lodging houses or the enginemen's barracks, were located around the system for the use of enginemen working long turns from their home sheds, commonly known as lodging turns. These allowed enginemen to rest before commencing the return working to their home territory. Many were restricted to enginemen and guards, and road motor drivers were not permitted to use them until the mid-1930s and in some locations, not until the war years. The majority were built by the pre-group companies before 1900, and this was reflected in the standards of accommodation available in some of these hostels. Only the modern ones, built in the 1930s at Upperby just prior to the war and at Kingmoor during the early war years, both in the Carlisle area, could be said to provide modern and homely comforts. The remainder were poor or very poor, being dark and with the minimum standards of hygiene, with facilities best described as frugal. The two new establishments around Carlisle supplemented the three pre-group hostels initially, and the earlier ones were then retired. For most men, the bed was to lie on in one's day clothes rather than a place where one could change into pyjamas for a good night's sleep, difficult at the best of times since most of them adjoined the locomotive depots. They were twenty four hour a day places, provided at the principal places where locomotive men changed places with a replacement crew for the next stage of the journey, at locations where there was a concentration of traffic. At the busiest locations, beds were often occupied around the clock, particularly during the dark war years. Drying rooms for enginemen's clothes and recreation rooms were also provided. One good feature was a constant supply of hot water, either piped from the adjacent engine shed boilers, or from boilers or large black-lead kettles within the hostel. Meals were adequate, rarely anything to write home about, but it must be remembered these were functional rather than prestigeous centres. Seldom, if ever, do we see the railway modeller providing a lodging house block as part of the motive power depot on a layout. Yet if one believes the image presented of a large shed, and the equally generous locomotive allocation to some model shed displays, then such a structure would not be out of place . . . food for thought.

The provision of drinking water at isolated locations was referred to in the standard instructions, merely to ensure that where such a piped facility was required, bubble drinking fountains rather than taps were to be fitted. Some isolated places had drinking water supplied in cans and carried by train.

Shunters' huts, yard cabins, platelayers' cabins and the like were scattered around the system to meet local needs, and most originated from the pre-LMS period. Standard designs were evolved to meet all future requirements, whether in new locations or as replacements for older obsolete structures, there being three main types:

Type 1 - 15ft. long x 10ft. 6in. wide x 8ft. rising to 8ft. 3in. high internally, with water supply and lavatory extension 6ft. x 9ft. for nine men, three per shift.

Type 2 - as Type 1, but without water supply and lavatory, for nine men, three per shift.

Type 3 - 11ft. long x 10ft. 6in. x 8ft. and 8ft. 3in. as above, without water supply and lavatory, for one or two men per shift.

Construction was of 9in. brickwork, with a smooth interior finish, this being painted in standard colours as for internal offices and similar. Most of the older huts were of wooden construction, with some utilizing the flakes or sections used for signal cabins but others being of sturdier timber boarding. Many are still in use today, a tribute to the craftsmanship and the seasoning of timber from those earlier decades.

Plate 10 The original enginemen's accommodation in Mill Sreet, Crewe, close to Crewe North locomotive shed. It was built in 1867 to provide sleeping accommodation for 42 men. This photograph was taken in 1969 after the hostel was closed; of interest are the ventilation covers along the ridge of the roof, and the bay window which is partly obscured by the wall in the centre foreground.

D. P. Rowland

Plate 11 A much larger hostel, built in 1897 in Gresty Road, Crewe, and located conveniently close to Crewe South locomotive shed, which was principally the freight engine depot in the Crewe area. Just visible to the right of the main building is the additional dormitory accommodation provided during World War II, when guards and road motor men working away from home were also permitted to use the facilities.

D. P. Rowland

Plate 12 A yard cabin interior, typical of many thousands of similar cabins located in goods and locomotive yards all over the system. Once the fire was lit they were quite snug, but many railwaymen would testify that some were like barns in winter, and after the weekend, hats and coats would not be taken off. Nevertheless, for the most part they were well looked after and kept clean and tidy ready for the next shift. This view should assist modellers in constructing a realistic interior for their yard cabin.

V. R. Anderson Collection

Early Locomotive Liveries

Plate 13 (below left) A Horwich 4-6-0 of L&YR Hughes design, built in 1923 and shown here in works 'photographic grey' livery. It has an interesting numberplate, of L&YR design but with 'LM&S Ry Co, Makers' at the top and 'Horwich 1923' on the lower edge. The small oval plate above the numberplate is the L&YR engine type, Class 8 in this case, with lining and panelling to the constituent company style. A considerable number of this class did not receive passenger livery immediately, and whilst it is assumed they entered traffic in black livery, it is possible they ran in the livery shown for a short period.

National Railway Museum

Plate 14 (below right) It is stated that No. 10433 was the first LMS locomotive. It was built by the L&YR (then part of the L&NWR) as engine No. 1662 and completed in December 1922. Its first day in traffic is recorded as 1st January 1923, hence the honour of being 'the first'. It went into service on the Horwich-Blackrod branch and was finished in a dark grey colour with LM&SR on the tender panels, and this livery corresponds closely to that shown in the previous plate. No. 10433 is shown in the first official style for the officially chosen 'lake' colouring, the decision having been taken in the spring or early summer of 1923.

National Railway Museum

The First Diesel Express Service in Great Britain

On 20th February 1933, the first express passenger service to be operated by diesel-electric power was inaugurated, running between Euston and the British Industries Fair site at Castle Bromwich on the outskirts of Birmingham, where a special platform had been erected in the grounds. The Armstrong-Shell express was a single car unit, with a Sulzer six cylinder diesel engine driving a main generator, with a driver's compartment at each end. There were Pullman type chairs for twelve passengers in two compartments and in addition to two toilet compartments, a well-equipped kitchen and pantry was provided. One novel feature in one of the pasenger compartments was a speedometer and journey progress indicator, which kept passengers informed by showing the point the car was passing progressively throughout the journey. Its maximum recorded speed was 70m.p.h. but it was regularly to be seen running at above 60m.p.h. - p.w.s. permitting. Armstrong Whitworth built the vehicle and Shell provided the light diesoleum oil on which it ran. Its fate, after the British Industries Fair ended is not known. It was an experimental vehicle, and whilst for twelve passengers per journey it could be considered an expensive vehicle in terms of track occupancy, the cost of fuel per mile run was stated to be 0.71d.

There were three Leyland four wheel railcars built in 1933, and two Coventry Pneumatic Railcar Co. vehicles in 1937. They were both introduced to services but only the initial prototypes were built, and they were not considered suitable as express units. The next major diesel experiment for passenger train operation was the 1938 three car unit.

Plate 15   The Armstrong-Shell express unit is seen at Nuneaton on 13th February 1933, prior to entering service on 20th February. The engine compartment ventilators and exhaust pipes with silencer units can easily be seen. The outward box appearance was generally similar to the LNER Tyneside 'Venturer' units.

National Railway Museum

Plate 16   Described as the 'latest thing on rails and first of its kind in Great Britain', this three car diesel light passenger unit was completed at Derby Carriage & Wagon Works early in 1938. It underwent trials on the Oxford to Cambridge line, and on a trial run from Euston to Tring and back, the unit attained a maximum speed of approximately 80m.p.h. Seating 164 passengers, it was powered by a Leyland engine, and direct assessment of this unit's performance was measured against the ordinary steam trains on the Oxford to Cambridge line. It also saw service on the Nottingham-Newark-Lincoln line, and from Leicester to Bedford. In official LMS journals, the livery is quoted as aluminium and post office red. In this view, taken in late 1938 or early 1939, the streamlined panels originally fitted between the bogies have been removed. In addition, oval buffer faces have been fitted to the original tube-like buffers, and the size of the originals can be seen on the buffer faces - but only at this end of the train. Another feature added during its period in traffic was the wire grid over the driving end windows.

National Railway Museum

Plate 17 An interior view of the three car diesel light passenger unit, looking from the driving cabin towards the toilet bulkhead. The seats were to a new design with reversible backs.

National Railway Museum

Plate 18 Soon after the delivery of the three car diesel light passenger unit shown in the two previous plates, the LMS placed in service with the Northern Counties Committee in Northern Ireland, a single unit diesel railcar, designed for operating main line intermediate services where sustained periods of high speed running were required. Also suitable for local services where rapid acceleration and deceleration were necessary between frequent stops, it followed the general outline and principal of the Michelin railcars, with the driving position elevated in a pod above the roof of the car. The body was constructed of teak frame with steel panels, and finished in an external livery of crimson lake with cream upper panels and the LMS crest on the side of each cab. The interior finish was fawn and dark brown rexine panelling with a white roof, and third class seating for eighty passengers comprised reversible back seats upholstered in blue moquette. The unit was No. 4 railcar in the NCC fleet, and it is seen here at Belfast North Road Station in April 1951, prior to departure for Ballymena, with what appears to be a modified livery. The guard's compartment was in the centre of the car.

T. J. Edgington

SPEND YOUR HOLIDAY MONEY WISELY

Half the fun of a holiday is thinking about it beforehand. Get the new edition of "Holidays by LMS" and begin planning your Holiday now.

"Holidays by LMS" not only gives you descriptions and illustrations of all the best resorts and all the most beautiful holiday districts, but includes a comprehensive list of hotels, boarding houses and apartments. A bumper six-pennyworth. From LMS Stations, Offices and Bookstalls.

ERO 41847
OP 3.

LMS SAVE TO TRAVEL SCHEME

NAME.....................................

ADDRESS.................................

....

....

WALLET FOR STAMP CARD AND VOUCHERS

Plate 19 The 'Save to Travel' scheme was introduced on 1st January 1936, and by the end of June that year more than 120,000 one shilling stamps had been purchased by intending travellers. The scheme had advantages for the railway company as they had a steady flow of income from passengers who were future rather than instant travellers, and therefore the Company had the benefit of monies which, in effect, were 'loans' or 'payments in advance'. The advantage for the passenger was that he did not have to pay up all at once for tickets. The one shilling stamps were on sale at all stations and were non-interest bearing, but once the stamp card with ten stamps was complete, it could be exchanged for a ten shilling voucher. This attracted interest at the rate of one halfpenny per month commencing from the month after issue, up to a maximum of sixpence per voucher, which was a twelve month investment. A folder or wallet was provided, in which the traveller could retain stamp cards and vouchers. It was considered a success in the early months of 1936, and the scheme was extended so that the promoters of guaranteed excursions could collect instalments and pay them into the Company, and for auxiliary ticket agents to have the scheme available for their clients.

Author's Collection

Holiday Contract Tickets

Plate 20 Holiday Contract 'Runabout' Tickets were issued in no less than 26 districts around the LMS system, covering the majority of the best known holiday resorts. The holders could travel as often as they wished during the seven day period of the ticket, and first and third classes were available. This North Wales district ticket was undoubtedly a bargain at fifteen shillings for a week of unlimited travel.

Author's Collection

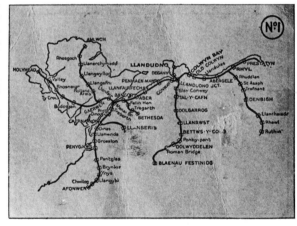

Plate 21 This is a maroon leather wallet designed to hold a season ticket, the details of which could be seen through a clear plastic window provided on the other side. The lettering is depressed into the leather, and even the stitching is maroon. These were provided free to holders of season tickets.

G. Foxley

Plate 22 The Holiday 'Runabout' area covered by the ticket in *Plate 20* included the Caernarvon and Llanberis branch line. This picturesque area created very little traffic for the normal branch passenger trains, so they were withdrawn in the early 1930s. A bus alternative was provided by the LMS-owned Crosville Bus Co., but only for one year, 1929/30. During the holiday season, however, excursion trains did run on the branch to link with the Snowdon Mountain Railway which ran from Llanberis, with an observation car provided. In this view, the former L&NWR saloon is resplendent in its new LMS livery, and a group of railway officials occupy the best seats. Passengers using these saloons, which also ran on other North Wales branch lines, were charged a supplementary fare.

British Railways

Excursion Traffic

In *LMS Miscellany, Volume I*, a number of excursion handbills were shown in *Plate 159*, and there were many hundreds of these issued each year to advertise untimetabled passenger workings. Events of all kinds attracted the attention of the LMS, from national exhibitions to football matches, and included theatre performances, holiday specials and localized agricultural shows. Single trains to such events accounted for most of the excursion traffic, but Blackpool Illuminations and international soccer matches were events which attracted thousands of people each year, and the LMS always provided a number of trains from different parts of the system.

Blackpool Illuminations traffic could claim to be the greatest attraction for the excursionists, with well over 1,100 long-distance special trains conveying more than half a million passengers each year. It was, of course, the longest running attraction and the 'lights' season ran from mid-September to the last week of October. Blackpool North Station carried most of the traffic, but there were also a number of excursion platforms alongside the main line terminus at Blackpool Central Station, situated almost beneath the tower.

An excursion with a difference would be an apt title for one such train which left Buchanan Street Station on Christmas Eve 1927, as the 'Gleneagles Dance Special'. First class carriages with Pullman restaurant cars made up the train, which left promptly at 6p.m. for the sixty mile journey, at the end of which the dancers were transferred the short distance from the station to the world-renowned Gleneagles Hotel. Luxury abounded in all ways and there was no shortage of patrons. The early hours of Christmas morning

echoed to the sound of this special train as it proceeded to return the tired partygoers to the now quiet city of Glasgow. This was perhaps one of the most notable excursions, but one single event which captured the attention of the nation was, of course, the Grand National steeplechase. For the race on 29th March 1930, no fewer than 43 trains headed for Aintree. From 7a.m. through to 11a.m. on the following day, a special train left some point on the LMS system every six minutes, and three of these were first class only specials from Euston. Vast quantities of food were prepared by the catering department and supplied for these trains.

The half-day excursions were very popular and, during the 1932 season, close on 5,000 such trains carried nearly two million excursionists, ranging from football enthusiasts to those who wished to do nothing more than explore some of the beauty spots around the country. Thomas Cook had commenced the excursion programme by train as long ago as 1841, and arrangements were made with the Midland Counties Railway and later the Midland Railway for special excursion trains to be run, and for Mr Cook to handle the booking arrangements. In those early years, the specials were not a lucrative source of income, and it was more through love for people rather than money that he regularly booked trains. LMS excursions were often billed by the Company as 'Cook's Excursions' but they were the ones which ran to places of interest rather than to special events, although there are examples where Cooks did sponsor trains to special events of national and, usually, annual interest.

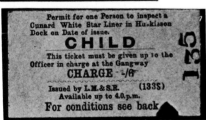

Plate 23   An excursion arrival at Wembley Central, comprising a mostly male gathering, which must indicate they are on their way to one of the football matches at Wembley Stadium in 1935. The carriages are a mixed assortment of two window stock with different rainstrips and torpedo vents which do not stand too proud of the carriage roof, which is often a mistake made by some modellers. The lamp to the bottom left corner of the picture is lettered 'Wembley for Sudbury'.

V. R. Anderson Collection

Plate 24   Rushworth's excursion to 'Radiolympia', in 1936, is seen passing Brinklow. Unusually, the train carries a large headboard, but few excursions were so adorned, other than the excursion reporting number which can be seen immediately beneath the chimney. Rushworths, presumably a radio company, may have been giving employees and customers a special day out.

G. Coltas

Plate 25 A special excursion, entering Lightcliffe Station, headed by ex-L&YR 0-6-0 No. 12194, with a Central Division reporting number of C894 carried on the smokebox and in the window of the first and last carriages. The reporting numbers clearly identified each rake of stock, and so prevented any confusion when the engine returned from the local shed at the destination, to pick up the rake in readiness for the return journey.

G. Coltas

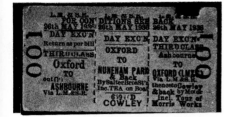

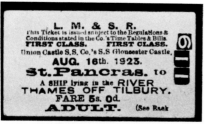

Plate 26 Street advertising, along railway-owned boundary walls, fences and poster boards, brought in additional revenue, and advertising agents were employed on a commission basis to maximize the use of these spaces. In this view, the LMS has taken the greater area to advertise its services, with Jacob's Cream Crackers being relegated to the spare portion. This was a roadway site beneath one of the many railway overbridges in the Manchester area.

National Railway Museum

Plate 27 (above)   An excursion advertising board, which is fastened to the station fencing, with a variety of offers for the Easter period of 1928.

National Railway Museum

Plate 28 (left)   A chalked excursion board, typical of many produced by station staff. The Lancashire Wakes Weeks were a source of additional traffic for the LMS with full-day, half-day and evening excursions always well patronized.

National Railway Museum

Plate 29 (below)   Blackpool Promenade, looking towards North Pier, with an enquiry office set up by the LMS to advertise excursions and deal with train enquiries, seen in the foreground. This must have been a 'plum' job - working on the seafront throughout the season, plenty of fresh air, meeting lots of people, to say nothing of being paid for a holiday job by the LMS. The whole office must have been quite eye catching, with the LMS crest on a white or pale cream background with a crimson (or black) base. The only thing missing is the LMS flag. Of the sign boards on top, one points to Talbot Road Station and the other to Central Station.

National Railway Museum

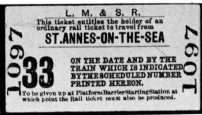

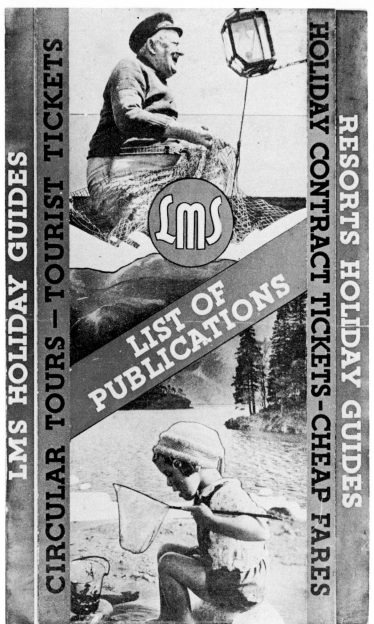

LMS HOLIDAY GUIDES

CIRCULAR TOURS—TOURIST TICKETS

LIST OF PUBLICATIONS

HOLIDAY CONTRACT TICKETS—CHEAP FARES

RESORTS HOLIDAY GUIDES

Plate 31 Two illustrations from the pamphlet.

L. Knighton Collection

Plate 30 Not only did the LMS produce a series of holiday guides and brochures to attract holiday-makers to travel LMS, they also had supplies of holiday resort brochures. These were produced individually by the resorts, and were available from the enquiry bureaux at principal stations or from the District Passenger Managers in England and Wales, or the Commercial Manager, Glasgow. More than two dozen resorts made brochures available, and this pamphlet provided the prospective holiday-maker with a full list of what was available from his local LMS office, to assist him in selecting the destination.

L. Knighton Collection

Examples of Excursion Tickets

LMS
1934 TRAVEL BARGAINS

1933 SAW AN ERA OF CHEAPER RAIL TRAVEL

•

IN 1934 THE LMS OFFERS YOU GREATER TRAVEL FACILITIES

•

MORE TRAINS FASTER TRAINS & BETTER TRAINS

•

HELP US TO HELP YOU ON YOUR HOLIDAY PROBLEMS

HOLIDAY-MAKERS · RAMBLERS · PARTY-ORGANISERS · ANGLERS · CLUBS, ETC.

TELL YOUR LOCAL LMS STATION-MASTER WHEN & WHERE YOU WANT TO GO & THE LMS WILL TAKE YOU THERE

(E.R.O. 53306)   Jowett & Sowry, Ltd., Printers, Leeds.

L. M. & S. R.
CIRCULAR TOUR No. 114
3rd CLASS
THE TICKET COLLECTOR MUST CAREFULLY DETACH THE TICKETS WHICH THEY HAVE TO COLLECT.
BURSLEM
0018

L. M. &
FOR CONDITIONS SEE BACK
CIRCULAR TOUR NO. 114 (2611)
BURSLEM TO OXFORD (LMS)
VIA L. M. & S. R. & BLETCHLEY
THIRD CLASS
0018

Messrs. Salter Bros' Steamer.
FOR CONDITIONS SEE BACK
L. M. & S. ISSUE
Available only while the Boat is running
CIRCULAR TOUR NO. 114 (2611)
This Ticket is issued by the L.M.& S.R.Co. as Agents for&on behalf of the SteamboatOwners, subject to the conditions printed on the back.
OXFORD TO KINGSTON
STEAMER
0018

This Ticket is NOT TRANSFERABLE
The Steamship Owners are not liable for loss of life or loss or injury to Passengers or their luggage from whatever cause arising.

L. M. & S. R.
FOR CONDITIONS SEE BACK
CIRCULAR TOUR NO. 114 (2611)
LONDON(Eus.) TO BURSLEM
Via Colwich or Norton B'ge & Stoke
THIRD CLASS
0018

Plate 32 (above) Circular tour ticket - the top section folds round the other tickets to form a ticket book arrangement.
G. Waite Collection

Penny-a-Mile And Land Cruises

New 'Penny-a-Mile' summer tickets were introduced by the four main line companies on 1st May 1933, and remained in force until 30th September. The new 'bargain' represented 'single-fare-and-a-third' travel, with the tickets being valid for one month, and there were no restrictions on when or where they could be used. They were an improvement over the previously available 'holiday return tickets' and tourist tickets, in that they were available for a month.

'Land Cruises' were another innovation of 1933, in that passengers could decide where and when they wished to travel outward, the route and places they wished to see or stay at and, the route they would take to reach home again. The LMS made all arrangements, including hotel or boarding-house accommodation for the requisite periods, and with the cheap summer tickets, charged an all-in fee for a 'Land Cruise'. Those wishing to book their own accommodation could also select the route and obtain the appropriate round trip ticket.

Cheap night travel was another special offer, for travel to the major holiday resorts, with special trains being laid on where the demand existed during the peak holiday periods.

It is a fact that the LMS, and the other companies, lost no time in offering special fare deals to woo passengers to use their services, in the face of increasingly severe competition from the motor coach operators in the 1930s.

Plate 33 (above) A handbill, supplied to most stations in the early months of 1934, extolling the offers available.

Author's Collection

The LMS Operations in Ireland

In Ireland, the LMS had substantial interests, these being:

Northern Counties Railway - wholly-owned and operated, with 280 miles and 52 chains of routes, of which some 77 miles and 73 chains were 3ft. gauge, including the 3ft. line from Londonderry to Strabane. Although this was wholly-owned by the NCC, it was operated by the County Donegal Railways Joint Committee.

Dundalk, Newry & Greenore Railway - wholly-owned, and from 1933 it was operated by the Great Northern Railway of Ireland, with which it connected at Dundalk and Newry.

The remaining interests in Ireland were a half share in the County Donegal Railways, a minority shareholding in the Great Northern Railway and a minority shareholding in the Great Southern Railway, all interests having been taken over from the pre-group constituent companies.

A history will not be attempted, but the inclusion of this section is intended to show that there was an LMS presence and, moreover, an LMS influence which can be identified from some of the locomotive and carriage designs which emanated from Derby and, to a lesser extent, from Crewe, albeit in pre-grouping days.

The NCC was the largest operation, and its main trunk route was from Belfast to Londonderry, 95 miles long before the Greenisland loop was built, when it then became 2¼ miles shorter. The Midland Railway had taken over the Belfast & Northern Counties Railway in 1903 and from then on, Midland influence was most noticeable.

There were a number of connecting points with other railways, these being located at Belfast, Antrim, Cookstown, Strabane, Londonderry and Ballyshannon.

In 1923, the Northern Counties Railway produced a net revenue of £122,472, dropping to £2,851 in 1926, rising thereafter each year to £21,669 in 1929, and in 1930, a deficit of £21,723 was recorded. The years up to 1935 each recorded deficits, only to turn around to a profit of £9,882 by the end of 1936.

Income from the County Donegal, the Great Northern and Great Southern was in the form of interest and dividends on investments, and for 1935 these were:

County Donegal	£ 7,217
Great Northern	£ 152
Great Southern	£ 11,655

Figures are not available for the Dundalk, Newry & Greenore Railway.

The Dundalk, Newry & Greenore Railway was isolated in the eastern border area, and was formerly part of the L&NWR interests, with connections with the Great Northern at Dundalk and Newry. Such was the length of the line that one could traverse the full mileage in a 73 minute journey time, leaving Dundalk on the 10.28a.m. stopping train to Greenore, arriving at 11a.m., changing to the Newry train leaving at 11.05a.m. and some 36 minutes later set foot on Bridge Street Station platform in Newry. In 1933, the Great Northern Railway took over the operation of the line, to achieve substantial economies. Much of the traffic was cattle movement, and the port of Greenore was a busy one for the export of livestock.

The accompanying photographs give a broad insight into LMS activities which were an important part of transportation in Ireland, but the Company also had seven important sea routes from the mainland, linking with the railway network at Londonderry, Larne, Belfast and a cargo route into Greenore.

On 6th January 1942 an important milestone was reached in the operations of the NCC, when substantial numbers of troops from the United States forces were disembarked in Northern Ireland, and these were carried by the NCC, together with equipment, to the ports for movement across the Irish Sea and into England and Wales.

The remaining activity by the Company was largely confined to LMS-appointed Directors to the Boards of the County Donegal Railways Joint Committee and the Great Southern Railway.

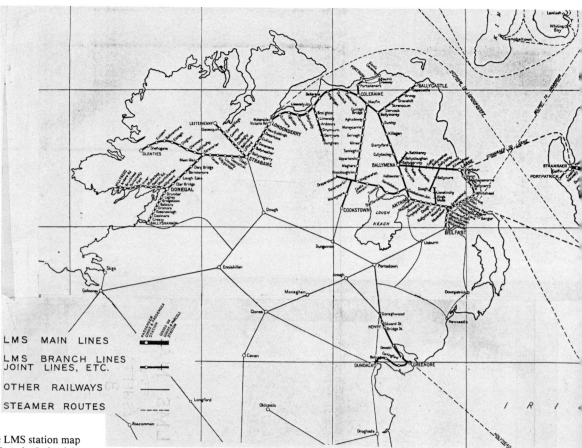

Plate 34 An extract from the LMS station map of 1939, showing the LMS lines in Ireland in schematic form.

Author's Collection

Plate 35 Greenore Station and the gateway to the Irish Sea. Although this photograph was taken in 1951 after the demise of the LMS, there is little evidence of change. A steamer is berthed and there is evidence, in the number of vans and containers in the yard, of some traffic but little more than a month after this picture was taken, the line was closed. The wider 5ft. 3in. gauge is perhaps most noticeable from the end-on view of the wagon nearest the camera, giving a somewhat squat appearance when compared with the British railway wagons. The fan of sidings is controlled by manually-operated point levers, and there appears to be but one set of point rodding in the picture, probably serving the crossover on the passenger platform line, along which a bunker-first tank engine is seen hauling a rake of carriages.

British Railways

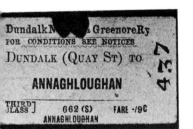

ate 36 Dated December 1951, this picture was ∍obably the last official one of Greenore Station taken closure time. There is much to interest the modeller of e Irish scene, including the platform surface bricks, e general shed construction, the L&NWR style notice-ards and the later LMS poster-boards. The seat in the ∍eground is of L&NWR origin, as is the refreshment ∍m facade beyond the buffers.

British Railways

Plate 37 The interior of Greenore goods warehouse; another official print taken at the time of closure. The construction of the roof is very similar to that of the station roof in the previous plate, with the addition of four pairs of lattice girders between the walls, each pair arranged in 'V' formation, and anchored to the sliding door frame to give strength. The sloping structures are tarpaulin frames, with one at each end of the shed and, in front of the nearest one is a stock of chain. The two hand barrows are of L&NWR standard large type.

British Railways

Plate 38 The front of Quay Street Station at Dundalk, with a board proclaiming the services available.

British Railways

Plate 39   Derby Carriage & Wagon Works, pictured in April 1924. This 57ft. eight compartment third corridor coach is complete and ready for movement to Belfast, and is standing on specially laid rails.

British Railways

Plate 40   Four 2-6-0 tender engines were built at Derby in 1933 for the NCC, and here, the first, No. 90, stands completed on a specially made piece of track. The rail is very similar to some of that used around 1850 on parts of the Midland Railway, and in fact some similarly sectioned rail was excavated a few years ago in Derby Carriage Works. The crest embellishes the cabside above the cast numberplate.

British Railways

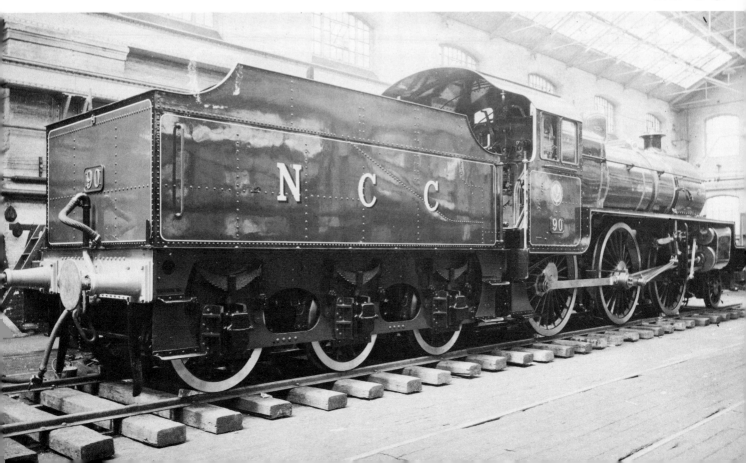

Plate 41 The engines were completed at Derby, and then partially stripped down to facilitate movement via Heysham to Belfast. Here the frame and boiler section is being lifted into the hold of the *S S Duke of Rothesay* on 6th July 1933, and for the journey will stand upon the sleeper packing laid out in readiness.

British Railways

Plate 42 The second of the four locomotives of Lot 178 was 2-6-4 tank No. 6, built at Derby in 1946, loaded and awaiting the journey to Heysham. There are three main sections plus wheels and the crate adjacent to the coal bunker, which probably carries the chimney, dome cover and other fittings.

British Railways

Plate 43 (left)   The Dundalk, Newry & Greenore carriage stock was turned out in the fully lined L&NWR livery and insignia throughout the LMS period, with a crest that bore more than a passing resemblance to the L&NWR device.

British Railways

Plate 44 (below) Not many passengers today can, or wish, to recall the six-a-side seating of the non-corridor stock, and this plate serves as a reminder of a typical compartment. This is a second class compartment in the Dundalk Newry and Greenore composite No. 2, and it is worth noting the moulded ceiling panels, the narrow high-backed seating and the handle beneath the picture, which one cranked over to have even a chance of the heating system responding. The narrow luggage rack is a reminder, at least to the author, that little more than a haversack or shopping bag would ride safely aloft and, if one valued one's life, cases were safer on the floor. Another feature lost in time is the heavy-duty leather strap, which enabled the passenger to open or close the droplight window.

R. Barr Collection

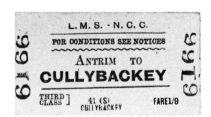

Plate 45 One of the NCC 3ft. gauge 2-4-2 tank engines No. 102, at Belfast in 1931 for repair, brought in on a 5ft. 3in. gauge wagon. The two non-driving axles have been removed. There are one or two interesting wagons in the background, carrying LMS and NCC lettering.

G. Coltas

Plate 46 Another 3ft. gauge tank, inside Belfast Shed in 1931. This is a former Belfast & Northern Counties Railway locomotive, with appropriate initials cast into the numberplate. Again the LMS crest is carried on the upper cab panels.

G. Coltas

Plate 47 No. 83, carrying the nameplates *Carra Castle*, which bear a strong resemblance to the Great Western nameplate pattern. The engine is one supplied from Derby Works between 1905 and 1908, and again the similarity to the Derby 2P locomotives is evident.

G. Coltas

Plate 48 No. 41, an altogether quaint 2-4-0 locomotive, fitted with cab protection sheet, seen with a passenger train at Belfast in July 1932.

G. Coltas

Plate 49 The Greenisland Viaduct built in 1933, bearing the initials LMS and NCC on either side of the date. When built, this was the largest reinforced concrete viaduct in the British Isles, and whilst LMS monies went into the project, it also attracted Government funds under one of the employment creation schemes. This viaduct was part of the loop between Bleach Green and Monkstown on the Belfast to Londonderry route, and when opened, track mileage was reduced by 2¼ miles.

R. Barr Collection

Named Trains

The most famous named trains on the LMS were the 'Royal Scot', the 'Coronation Scot' and 'The Irish Mail', this latter train having the distinction of being the oldest named train. The L&NWR had commenced 'The Irish Mail' service on 1st August 1848 with the 8.45p.m. train from Euston to Chester, with the mails then being handed on to the Chester & Holyhead Company for the journey to the Irish boat at Holyhead. The section between Bangor and Llanfair was by road mail coach. The 'Scotch Express' was the Midland's principal train.

In July 1927, the LMS recognized the publicity value in bestowing names on the principal expresses, the so-called 'crack trains', and they introduced a number of new ones. The names were advertised in the timetables, and a nameboard was carried on each carriage, but so far as can be ascertained, the engines did not carry headboards. The one train which was quite unmistakable was, of course, the 'Coronation Scot', with the sleek streamlined engine and carriages finished in a new mid-blue livery with four silver bands running the length of the train. This was the pride of the line, from its introduction on 5th July 1937 until August 1939, when it was taken out of service at the outbreak of war and, of course, it did not need a headboard. The train ran from new with the 'Coronation Scot' title painted on the carriages, and there were three rakes of carriages for this service. Sometime thereafter, separate nameboards were added.

On some lines, individual trains were given titles which may not have been widely known outside the locality, and into this category would come titles such as 'The Tutbury Jinny', by which the branch line trains between Burton-on-Trent and Tutbury were always known. There were also other similar local names.

The following is a list of the principal named trains:

Named Train	Route	Date Introduced
'The Belfast Boat Train'	Euston to Fleetwood (Belfast Boat)	—
'The Blackpool & Fylde Coast Express'	Blackpool (Central) to Euston	—
'The Blackpool Club Train'	Blackpool to Manchester (Victoria)	—
'The Bon-Accord'	Glasgow (Buchanan St.) to Aberdeen	1938
'The Business Man's Train'	Glasgow (Central) to Euston (overnight)	—
'The Canadian Pacific'	Euston to Liverpool (Landing Stage) to connect with Canadian Pacific liners	—
'The Comet'	Euston to Manchester (London Road)	1932
'The Coronation Scot'	Euston to Glasgow (Central)	1937
'The Devonian'	Bradford to Paignton	1927
'The Fast Belfast'	Glasgow (St. Enoch) to Stranraer	—
'The Granite City'	Glasgow (Buchanan St.) to Aberdeen	—
'The Hebridean'	Inverness to Kyle of Lochalsh	—
'The Isle of Man Boat Express'	Glasgow (Central) to Ardrossan	—
'The Irish Mail'	Euston to Holyhead	—
'The Isle of Man Boat Train'	Manchester (Victoria) to Fleetwood (Douglas Boat)	—
'The Irishman'	Glasgow (St. Enoch) to Stranraer	—
'The John O' Groat'	Inverness to Wick (summer only)	—
'The Lakes Express'	Euston to Windermere	—
'The Blackpool, Southport & Lakes Express'	Euston to Windermere (with sections to Southport and Blackpool)	—
'The Lancastrian'	Euston to Manchester (London Road)	1927
'The Lewisman'	Kyle of Lochalsh to Inverness	—
'The Llandudno Club Train'	Manchester (Exchange) to Llandudno	—
'The Mancunian'	Manchester (London Road) to Euston	—
'The Manxman'	Euston to Liverpool (summer only)	—
'The Merseyside Express'	Euston to Liverpool (Lime St.)	1927
'The Midday Scot'	Euston to Glasgow (Central)/Edinburgh (Princes St.)	1927
'The Night Scot'	Euston to Glasgow (Central)	1927
'The Orcadian'	Inverness to Wick	1936
'The Palatine'	St. Pancras to Manchester/Liverpool	—
'The Peak Express'	St. Pancras to Manchester (Central)	—
'The Pines Express'	Manchester (London Road) to Bournemouth	1927
'The Royal Highlander'	Euston to Inverness/Aberdeen	—
'The Royal Scot'	Euston to Glasgow (Central)/Edinburgh (Princes St.)	1927
'The Saint Mungo'	Glasgow (Buchanan St.) to Aberdeen	1938
'The Scotch Express'	9.15a.m. St. Pancras to Edinburgh (Waverley)	—
	9.30a.m. St. Pancras to Glasgow (St. Enoch)	—
'The Sunny South Express'	Manchester (London Road) to Eastbourne and Brighton	—
'The Thames-Clyde Express'	St. Pancras to Glasgow (St. Enoch)	1927
'The Thames-Forth Express'	St. Pancras to Edinburgh (Waverley)	1927
'The Tinto'	Glasgow (Central) to Carlisle	pre 1923
'The Ulster Express'	Euston to Fleetwood (later Heysham)	1927
'The Welshman'	Euston to North Wales (various points)	—
'The West Coast Postal'	Night mail train from Euston (split for various points in Scotland)	—
'The Windermere Club Train'	Windermere to Manchester (Exchange)	—
'The Yorkshire Express'	1.20p.m. St. Pancras to Bradford	—
'The Yorkshireman'	Bradford to St. Pancras	—

In addition, a number of expresses were given titles of a somewhat secondary nature, and the following are examples:

'The Sheffield Express'
'The Edinburgh–Gourock Express'   10.50a.m. St. Pancras to Sheffield
'The Crewe–Llandudno Express'

Plate 50 A poster advertisement for the 'Sunny South Express', which was a train from Manchester (London Road), to which was added through carriages from Liverpool (Lime Street), at Crewe. Through carriages from Birmingham and Coventry were added at Rugby, and a Northampton carriage was added at Willesden Junction. The train then proceeded over the West London line through Kensington and Clapham Junction, and on to the Southern to the South Coast resorts it served.

National Railway Museum

Plate 51 What better engine than No. 6245 *City of London* to head the 'Centenary Express', commemorating the 100th Anniversary of the 10a.m. London to Glasgow express service. Although this event took place on 16th February 1948, it was but 47 days out of the LMS period. Appropriately, although actually they had no other option, the engine and train were in full LMS livery of 1946 black for the non-streamlined 'Coronation' and Crimson Lake for the train. From this date, the 10a.m. service once again officially became the 'Royal Scot', but the name had been used unofficially on this service throughout World War II.

V. R. Anderson

Refreshment Rooms and Tea Rooms

Plate 52 The glazed brick and tile interior of the refreshment room at Rugby, pictured in December 1945, still well-appointed and reflecting the more affluent past rather than the end of war utility. LMS poster art adorns the walls, but the table accoutrements were probably a mixture of L&NWR and LMSR items. This was a full service category 'A' establishment.
V. R. Anderson Collection

Plate 53 The railbar at London's Euston Station was geared to meet the requirements of a different clientele, during the late war period.
V. R. Anderson Collection

Railway tea has long featured in the repertoire of the sta comedian and the barrack-room joker, but it is a fact that wh suits one person's taste doesn't please another. Just how ma cups or pots of tea have been served up by the railways is matter of conjecture, but the LMS had 134 dining, refreshme or tea rooms, and the combined total must have been measur in billions of cups. The principal offering through the stati facilities was a meal in a basket, with most establishme offering hot or cold meals, whether it be breakfast, lunchec tea or dinner. The LMS published lists with each locati marked in relation to the service available, be it A, B, C, D E. These took the following form:

A Breakfast, luncheon and dinner baskets (hot or colc tea baskets, or tea trays. Minimum of 45 minutes not required for hot food.

B Breakfast baskets (containing cold ham etc., with tea coffee), luncheon baskets, hot or cold, and minimum one hour's notice for hot luncheons. Dinner baskets cc taining cold food only, tea baskets or tea trays.

C Breakfast, luncheon and dinner baskets, containing cc food only. Tea baskets or tea trays only.

D Tea baskets or tea trays only.

E Not under LMS management.

Seventeen locations were marked 'E', with four in Engla (at Bristol, Dalston Junction, Southend and Uttoxeter) a one in Wales at Rhyl, and the remaining twelve in Scotla (at Aberdeen, Oban, Perth (General), Airdrie, Ballachulis Beattock, Dalmally, Guthrie, Kentallen, Lairg, Lockerbie a Newton Stewart). All were establishments which were n under LMS management, (list relates to 1935).

Four establishments were open for the summer season on at Aviemore, Windermere Station, the Lakeside Pavilion a at Bowness Pier.

Orders were taken in advance for hot meals, which we available to take on to trains without extra charge. For tho who wished to place an order at the commencement of the journey for collection en route, the Company provided a fr telegram service to place the order. A bottle of wine, or inde a half bottle, could also be made available.

A major headache for both the staff and for the Compa was the loss of crockery, cutlery and trays as a result of the items being taken on to trains. Although the majority we never misappropriated by the passengers, a cup handed out Crewe and left to be picked up at Euston, Glasgow or Der was no longer any use to the staff at Crewe. Larger stocks we therefore maintained at each location.

In every establishment, a notice proclaimed 'any passeng may obtain a glass of drinking water free of charge'.

Not only did the LMS carry enormous quantities of pottery-ware from the Stoke-on-Trent area to all parts of the country, it was also a sizeable purchaser of pottery items for its own use. Plates of all sizes, cups, saucers, cream and gravy jugs, to name but a few of the items, were all required to enable the hotels, refreshment rooms, dining cars, sleeping cars and staff canteens to operate. All items carried the Company identity letters as a safeguard against wholesale losses through theft, but the presence of these markings served also as a reminder to those using the various items of simply the LMS.

There were a number of suppliers in the Potteries, and it would indeed be surprising if any of the companies in the pottery industry had not, at some time, supplied the LMS. Whether any recognition of traffic consigned by rail from these companies was reciprocated in the way of orders for supplies is not known, but this could have been a factor in where they bought requirements.

Some of the hotels were permitted special pattern designs on crockery, and these items were often of a better quality than those used on the train. Few records exist of the vast quantities which must have been required during the twenty five year period of the Company, but it is reported that the large hotels would prepare as many as 2,000 meals each day when major events were staged at or near an LMS hotel. This volume would involve as many as 16-20,000 items in all to be required in stock.

The inventory for a dining car was as follows:

(Maximum 36 in one car, additional seated in adjoining car)

	20 seats	56 seats
Glass	20 pieces	136 pieces
China	302 pieces	687 pieces
Plate	260 pieces	667 pieces

(The twenty seat dining saloons were of pre-group origin)

There were between 175 and 200 services with LMS dining car accommodation operating each day, with a minimum staff on each vehicle of seven, including one conductor, four assistants, one cook and an assistant cook. Crockery breakages had to be accounted for when replacements were required from the catering service stores.

Plate 54 (left) The bottom of a cream jug, which was specially supplied to the Company.

Author's Collection

Plate 56 (below) Two similarly shaped cups, with the earlier one on top. Both have LMS depicted in red, not opposite the handle, but offset slightly to the 'front' for a right-handed person using the cup. There are markings on the underside on the lower cup only, and these are in green. Remember these thick cups? Rumour had it that they withstood dropping from trains.

G. Foxley Collection

Plate 55 (right) A few examples of plates and saucers:
1. A 6in diameter LMS saucer in red, made by A. G. R. & Co. Ltd.
2. An 8½in. LMS plate in black with Mintons crest and 11-29 written in black on the underside.
3. A 5¾in. LMS saucer in black, made by Swinnertons of Staffordshire which is marked on the underside.
4. A 6in. LMS green and blue saucer, with a marking on the underside that reads Chodziez, MAKE IN POLAND. Surprising the LMS should go abroad perhaps, but it could be due to either price or an English manufacturer sub-contracting the job. The lettering too is in green and blue, not the usual black or red.
5. A 6in. saucer, on which the underside markings shown are in black, there being no markings on the top surface.
6. An 8¼in. plate or shallow dish, with no markings on the top surface.
7. A 4in. diameter sugar bowl. The underside markings shown are in black, and a blue sea-horse marking on the side is just visible on the rim of the picture at the top.

Item number four appears to be the only post-war manufactured item shown, with the remainder believed to be of pre-war production.

G. Foxley Collection

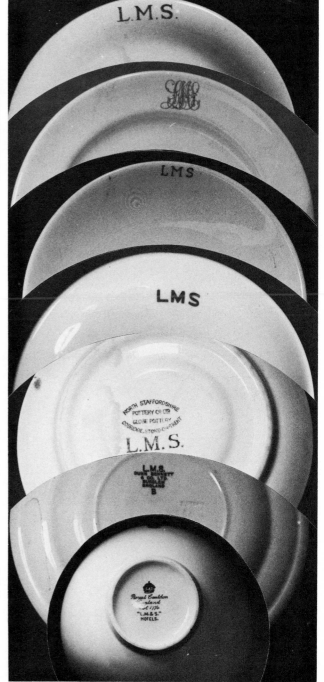

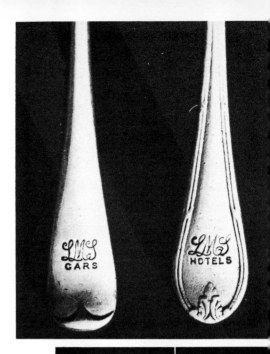

Plates 57, 58, 59 & 60 Yet more LMS markings, this time on cutlery items. The third fork has the lettering stamped the opposite way to the remainder, possibly intended to impress the person sitting at the opposite place setting to the user. The fourth spoon is marked 'RR', which denotes restaurant rooms issue. Most of the principal Sheffield cutlers supplied the Company, and most of the pre-war cutlery for the hotels and dining cars was silver plate. The largest spoon is marked 'Elkington plate' on the underside, whilst the next one is a Butler Sheffield plastic-handled spoon.

G. Foxley Collection

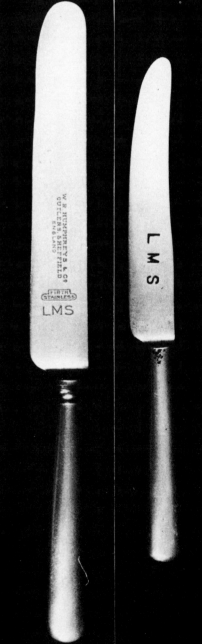

Drinking glasses, inkwells, beer bottles, medical bottles and, of course, carriage windows, all came from the glass industry in vast quantities, and, as with virtually all other movable items, evidence of LMS ownership was indestructibly marked on each item.

Plate 62 (right) A desk inkwell, with a 'W' mark on the base. Standing 2¾ in. high with a 3¼ in. diameter base, it was a reminder of the pre-ballpen days when pen and ink was the order of the day, and handwriting required no apology. Even pen nibs and the pen holder were marked with LMS.

G. Foxley Collection

Plate 61 (below) A 5¾ in. high glass, for fruit juices and soft drinks.

G. Foxley Collection

Plate 63 (right) A half-pint beer bottle with embossed lettering.

Author's Collection

Wear and Tear

Moving mechanical parts are bound to wear in time, and through a constant inspection and replacement programme, both on a regular basis at the motive power depots and during visits for minor or general overhauls at the works, the effects of wear on the efficiency of the locomotive was kept to a minimum. The amazing thing about a railway locomotive is that the tyre, which is a small section of metal, is sufficient to keep a very heavy mechanical contraption with an even heavier load on a straight and comparatively narrow piece of raised metal, in other words the rail. Do you recall, during those unforgettable shed visits, the grinding and screeching as a locomotive moved on tight radius curves or through badly worn sets of points? These noises were evidence that some wear on the tyres and rails was unavoidable. Faults in the composition of metals through the presence of particular chemicals in incorrect quantities, or through defects in casting, could give rise to failures in service if they were not detected during the processing or machining stages. Engine failures, for whatever reasons, were not uncommon in the steam era, and indeed it would be wrong to suggest they were a thing of the past. These failures were mostly the result of rigid inspection procedures designed to ensure that if an engine was in traffic, there was every reason to believe it would perform with the utmost safety for passengers, staff and equipment. The following two plates illustrate wear and tear.

Plate 65 An axlebox which has been severely damaged in traffic, possibly as a result of being badly fitted in the first place.

British Railways

Plate 64 (above) A driving wheel, from 'Coronation' class Pacific, No. 6247 *City of Liverpool*, showing the results of a faulty tyre casting which was undetected until the cracks appeared in traffic. The wheels and tyres were machined to very fine tolerances, and the tyres were heat expanded in gas rings, then shrunk-cooled on to the wheel centre to ensure a tight fit, before final tyre profiling. This crack may well have resulted through stress finding the weak point in the casting.

British Railways

Plate 66 The scrapping of locomotives by British Rail in the last few years up to the end of steam has been much lamented, but the inevitable fate for steeds of the iron road has been a fact of life since the railways began. The LMS had a vigorous standardization policy, which saw a considerable number of classes of engine disappear in a relatively short period, but this was perhaps acceptable and caused a good deal less comment because the replacements for the old engines were also steam engines. The replacements were, for the most part, larger in size and with greater power than their predecessors, and who can argue that the 'Royal Scot' and the 'Princess Royal' class locomotives and the Streamliners captured the imagination simply because they were capable of hauling longer trains at greater speeds. Locomotive works were essentially of a cluttered nature, and this view of the scrapping ground at Derby Works in 1936 is no exception. The remnants of so many engines were left to await reuse either as ready parts to keep others of the same class working, or as lumps of metal for the foundry. The only identifiable locomotive is the one on the right, which is a Drummond 0-6-2 tank from the Glasgow & South Western Railway, scrapped after a working life of less than twenty years. No. 16925 was its second LMS number, after the class as a whole had 500 added to the first allocated numbers in 1926 when, for example, 16425 became 16925. One memory of Derby Works in the late 1940s is the vast collection of locomotive domes which occupied part of the scrapping ground. The buildings are those used; on the left is the paint shop, and the remainder are machine and erecting shops, all of Midland Railway origin and in unaltered condition.

W. Potter

Scrapyard

Plate 67 The locomotive was not the only reason for this photograph, as there is a quantity of scrap brake-shoes, locomotive springs and fire-bars heaped ready for disposal. The small sack truck, which can be seen to the left of the scrap, is lettered 'MP'. Most Midland examples were lettered 'MR', but there is no evidence to suggest this was anything other than 'MP'. The picture was taken at Hasland Shed in 1930, with Johnson Midland Class 2P, No. 506 standing ahead of an ex-Midland Class 1P 0-4-4T, No. 1238.

G. Coltas

Plate 68 An ex-L&NWR electric motor coach, pictured in fully lined livery at Wolverton Works Yard, in August 1956. More than eight years after nationalization, the train is in the livery it received prior to World War II, some thirty years earlier.

F. W. Shuttleworth

Docks, Harbours and Wharves

The Company had substantial investments in both dock and harbour premises, and passenger and freight steamer fleets were centred on the various ports. All were well-equipped, and were instrumental in capturing much of the sea traffic from the United Kingdom mainland for the Company.

The following concerns were owned by the LMS:

	Length of quay in feet (1929)	Tonnages handled (1929)
England and Wales		
Barrow Harbour and Wharf	19,602	491,684
Deganwy Wharf	660	Nil
Fleetwood - Harbour	4,065	
- Wyre Docks	4,878	567,798
Foryd Wharf	324	1,800
Garston Docks	8,016	2,197,693
Gravesend Floating Stages	321	3,843
Heysham Harbour	4,100	291,562
Holyhead Harbour	7,467	376,798
London - Chelsea Dock (Jointly leased with the GWR)	695	28,947
- Poplar Docks	3,474	325,357
Morecambe Harbour	2,110	No traffic-private yard
Tilbury Floating Stage	300	3,940
Widnes Dock	894	7,292
	56,906	4,296,714
Scotland		
Ayr Harbour	7,560	1,565,305
Bowling Harbour	1,200	80,668
Fairlie Pier	280	2,884
Gourock Pier	2,286	11,322
Grangemouth Docks	16,092	3,735,213
Kentallen Pier	64	31
Kyle of Lochalsh Pier	835	19,532
Largs Harbour	630	421
Oban Pier	1,100	32,288
Renfrew Wharf	350	1,013
Stranraer East Pier	1,190	47,197
Troon Harbour	6,160	363,293
Wemyss Bay Pier	1,304	9,162
	39,051	5,868,329
Totals	95,957 feet	10,165,043 tons

Plate 69 Stalbridge Dock, which was part of the Garston Docks complex at Liverpool, with *S S Puriri* moored alongside in June 1945. Travelling cranes straddle the tracks and there is a fair assortment of wagons and containers in the picture, nearly all in pre-1936 livery. The wagon to the right appears to have brakes on one side only, a practice declared illegal from 1st January 1939.

British Railways

Plate 70 When Huskisson Dock at Liverpool was bombed in 1940, the offices were damaged beyond use, and this former Midland Railway inspection saloon, LMS No. 45035, was removed from the underframe and used as a replacement. Although this photograph was taken in late 1957, the body still carried the LMS lined livery, albeit in faded condition. The three railwaymen are in typical attire, with long waterproof aprons and open-necked shirts without collars, whilst the man on the right has the normal jacket beneath a waterproof outer top.

F. W. Shuttleworth

Plate 71 (above)   A hive of activity in this view of Fleetwood Docks, t
entire area being owned and operated by the LMS. Docks were an importa
part of the Company's services, adding substantial revenue in exchange fo
variety of facilities. Coal was transported to the mechanical handling pla
at the docks, for bunkering into the trawlers, of which there were large flee
Plentiful supplies of ice were also taken on board, and the incoming trawl
brought fish catches to the wholesale market place, which centred on t
covered shed accommodation. The bulk of fish traffic was then consigned
rail in specially built vans and containers. Slipways were also provided by t
Company, for use by trawler owners when repairs or refits were necessa
Large sums of money were invested in new equipment, in order to mainta
facilities befitting the most important fishing port on the West Coast.
1937, six giant electrically-operated coaling plants were erected at Fleetwoo
three serving the fish dock and three the Wyre Dock. Each plant could c
two trawlers simultaneously with 160 tons of coal, and complete the j
within two hours twenty minutes, a big change from the earlier crane a
bucket methods. An extensive network of rail tracks can be seen in this vi
with, in the foreground, trains of fish vans and a number of private ow
wagons. The two private-owner wagons at the right-hand end of the near
row appear to be from Dalton Main Colliery of Rotherham.

V. R. Anderson Collect

Plate 72 (below)   Another dockside scene, this time showing the Gravesend
vehicle landing stage for the ferry service to Tilbury, although the building
carries the title of Goods and Cattle Station.

British Railways

Dredgers

A far from glamorous group of craft which were owned by the Company were the dredgers, and they performed an even less glamorous but, none the less, very important role in keeping the LMS ports open. In tidal waters, the estuaries through which the boats passed became silted up, and if they were not cleared to a sufficient depth, then they would soon become impassable to all but the smallest of craft. There were three basic types of dredger. The first had a continuous chain of buckets, which scooped sand from the bed of the channel and emptied it into the dredge tank suspended beneath the keel of the vessel, before repeating the process, scoop after scoop. The dredge tank was then taken to deep water and emptied through bottom opening doors during low tide periods. The second method of dredging was the single grab type, which was more suited for the areas close to landing piers and dock gates. There were also the suction dredgers, for use close to landing stages or lock gates. Ferguson Bros. Ltd. of Port Glasgow were specialist dredger builders, and supplied several craft to the LMS, mostly the continuous bucket type. Three identical vessels built by Ferguson's in the 1926-1930 period were *Garstonia* for Garston Docks, the *Carronwater* for Grangemouth, the *Piel* for Barrow.

The men who worked these vessels had one important benefit over their counterparts on the revenue-earning services, in that they were allowed weekends off duty. But many were required to sleep on board during the week, so that round the clock dredging could be carried out. It was a never ending task, both tide in and tide out, and with each tide movement, some of the areas on the sea bed would soon have fresh deposits of sand. On and on these craft worked, a monotonous but vital service to the steamship operations of the Company.

Plate 73 (above) A picture of a grab hopper type 'pick-me-up' dredger, which was allocated to Holyhead. It is shifting a single bucket of silt to add to the tons already in the tank seen in *Plate 74*. A steam-driven hoist is operated by the weight carried by the chain, and the jaws of the hoist are released by the cable. This view is taken close to the landing stage at Holyhead, which can be seen on the left.

British Railways

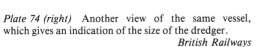

Plate 74 (right) Another view of the same vessel, which gives an indication of the size of the dredger.
British Railways

Plates 75 & 76   Views of two newly-constructed dredgers, the first being *Carronwater*, which was put into use at Grangemouth Docks and *Piel*, which worked in the channel near to Barrow-in-Furness. Both were equipped with masses of machinery, cables and heavy gear, and were put into service within a few months of each other early in 1927.

Author's Collection

Derby Signal Works

A view, alongside the River Derwent, of the former Midland Railway works, portions of which were built in 1872 and modernized in 1912. Most of the signal frames, posts and parts were manufactured here, and the works continued in operation until closure in 1932, when the patterns and stocks were transferred to Crewe. The stock list of parts numbered around 12,000 items.

In addition to looking after all signal requirements for the Midland Division of the LMS, it was also responsible for the manufacture of goods cranes, hoists, lifts, bridge parts, wagon traversers, field gates, lifting chains and tackle of all sorts. Rather surprisingly perhaps, repairs to the Company's fleet of dredgers also came under its jurisdiction. A narrow gauge railway system was in operation within the shops.

Plate 77 The former Midland Railway works, viewed from across the River Derwent.

G. Waite Collection

Plate 78 What appears to be a 125 lever frame, under construction in March 1928. Frames were built up and tested prior to dismantling for transportation to the required signal cabin site. The 125 figure is taken from the chalked number on the end lever, it being impossible to count beyond about eighteen levers. The small maker's plate was added to each end of every frame constructed from 1925 onwards.

G. Waite Collection

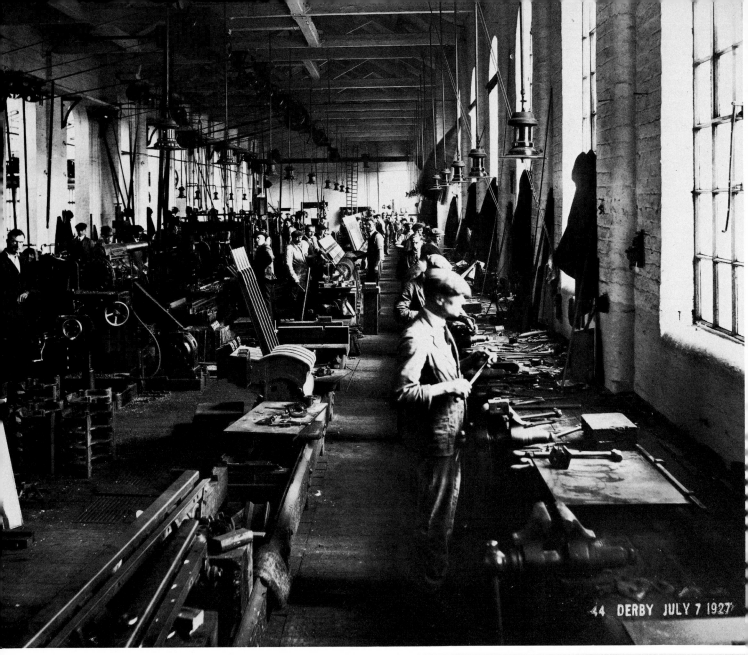

44 DERBY JULY 7 1927

Plate 79 Another interior view of the machine and assembly shop, showing a variety of equipment and tools. The small five lever frame in the centre has a smaller housing than that in the previous plate. Note the rather primitive, but none the less effective, belt drive arrangement, operated from a centre spindle attached to the rafters. This view was taken in the summer of 1927.

G. Waite Collection

Plate 80 A turn-over pattern frame, with seven levers, marked for a level crossing location. From left to right, the seven levers are for hand gate 'down' side, hand gate 'up' side, road gates, 'up' distant, 'up' home, 'down' home and 'down' distant.

G. Waite Collection

Take your Car by Rail

and avoid the fatigue of a lengthy journey by road.

Special Cheap Rates for accompanied Motor Cars.

Full particulars from any LMS Station Master.

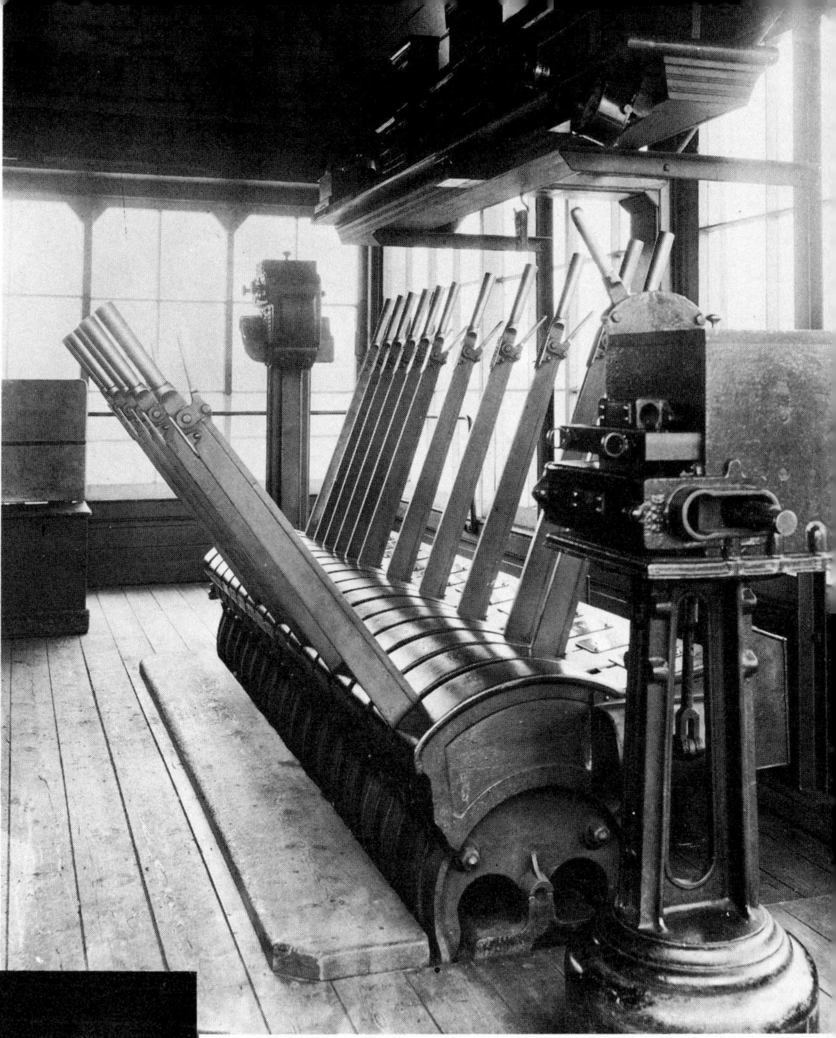

Plate 81 The interior of a Midland signal cabin, showing a Derby frame in use.

G. Waite Collection

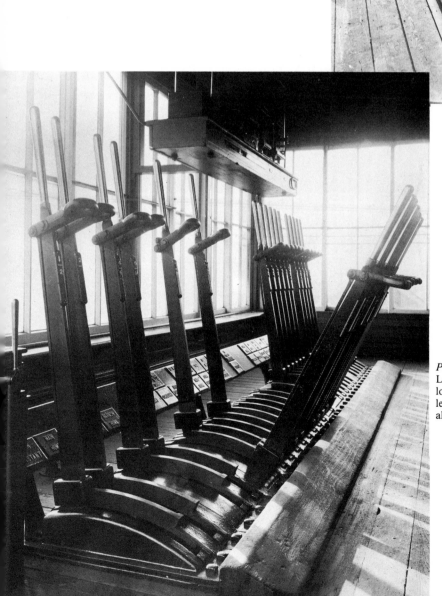

Plate 82 In contrast to the last plate is this picture of an L&NWR signal cabin interior, showing a different type of locking arrangement. The catch blocks, at the base of the levers, were raised by pushing down the catch handle, thus allowing the lever to be moved.

G. Waite Collection

Signalling

The technicalities of railway signalling cannot be covered in these notes, but appreciation of what the LMS did about signalling is more easily portrayed.

The constituent companies had met their signalling obligation either manufacturing the various components themselves, or purchasing them fr signalling contractors, of which there were several. The L&NWR, the Midland a the L&YR all had signal works manufacturing to their own designs, whilst remainder used a variety of commercially available equipment.

A variety of equipment was therefore in use in the early years of the LMS, a some early steps towards standardization were introduced. The L&YR works Horwich was closed, with patterns for signal parts being transferred to Crewe. Furness, Maryport & Carlisle and North Stafford railways commenced using L&NWR equipment in the early years, until standard LMS equipment beca available. It was well nigh impossible to attempt to change the entire equipment say nothing of the enormous cost involved, so standard LMS equipment therefore used in new installations, where improvements were undertaken, or wh renewal of old equipment became necessary. The greater part of the pre-gro equipment remained in use throughout the LMS period.

The LMS signal works at Derby was closed in 1932, and production of sign and locking frames was transferred to Crewe. A small signal works at Irvine Scotland was maintained, to cater for the Northern Division maintenance a renewal requirements.

Safety was the overriding factor which made signals a requirement on railways, and the first semaphore signal was used in 1841 on the London Blackwall Railway. The principle of the signalling block system was that the was considered as blocked with the signals at 'danger', and to allow passage, signal arm had to be moved to a 'clear' position. The first semaphore had been signal arm at horizontal for 'danger', and at 'clear', the arm slotted into the post dropping downwards. The lower quadrant signal arms, in use by the Grouping, w an improvement in as much as they were dropped from the horizontal by about degrees to show 'clear', but there were dangers in this system. If the signal w affected due to an an equiment failure or build-up of ice or snow on the arm could accidently drop into a 'clear' position.

In 1919, a committee of signal engineers met to consider designs for a new sig arm, with the upper quadrant system being the one chosen. It had to be raised give the 'clear' green aspect, and in the event of equipment failure, it would rem level at 'danger'.

Whilst a large number of signal posts had been painted white by the pre-group companies, there were also considerable numbers which, in photographs, appea black. During World War I, the Midland experimented with square creosoted po and for some years this practice was also adopted by the LMS. In fact, the Comp also undertook experiments with round creosoted posts and they were brought i more general use with the upper quadrant signals, the Company achieving finan benefits from using round timbers.

There were other signal innovations including, in 1932, speed signals, which only indicated the road clear, but how fast the driver should proceed, and examp of these were introduced to the Mirfield area widening scheme.

In 1935, steel signal posts were introduced as standard, tubular steel being u for signals less than 30ft. high, and lattice steel posts for signals which were taller Scotland, lattice signals had been in use for many years.

Colour light signals were progressively introduced on high density suburban lin and in major resignalling and track improvement schemes. In the Manchester a scheme of 1929, there were some interesting combinations of colour light a semaphore signals. Three aspect colour light distants with two yellow and a gr light were fitted below some of the home semaphores and four aspect runn signals, replaced semaphores in some locations. Yet another variation was circular cluster colour light, in either four or three aspect, which featured at so bracket signal locations.

The following plates illustrate some of the signal variations seen on the LMS.

Plate 84 The first upper quadrant signal, erected in the Derby Signal Works Yard in 1927, using a square creosoted post. Both arms appear to be painted red, but it is probable that the distant arm yellow was not picked out on the film plate used, so both appear to be the same colour. It was not until the Ministry of Transport introduced a requirement, in 1925, that distant signals were henceforth to be painted in yellow, with a black chevron on the face. Prior to this, they had been red with a vertical white band, as shown in some of the following prints.

G. Waite Collection

Plate 85 A standard gantry, erected at Derby Junction and photographed on 29th June 1932. Again the distant arms appear to be the same colour as the home signal arms, but with a black chevron, which is hardly discernible in this print. Repainting of distant arms to yellow commenced in 1929, and the film emulsion used for the picture has not picked out the colour differences.

G. Waite Collection

Plate 86 Shirebrook Junction, on 20th February 1929, showing an interesting balance weight arrangement installed for the double wire points, to enable the working of the Welbeck Colliery branch. The finial is of Midland origin, and the corners of the post were very slightly rounded off the square.

G. Waite Collection

80 DERBY APL 8 1925

Plate 87 A bank of ground signals, set up in the signal works yard and photographed in 1925. The picture was taken to record the experimental livery which was applied to the installation. A more interesting feature of this picture is the tall signal post, which appears to have four home arms fitted. Close examination suggests that there may have been four posts, each with one arm in direct line with the camera position.

G. Waite Collection

Fog and Snow Signalling Equipment

Fog is not so prevalent these days, largely because of the various 'clean air' measures instituted in recent years. In the steam era of railways, particularly in the industrialized areas, the general industrial smog was released into the atmosphere, and damp conditions seemed to create fog quite often.

As a result, trains were slowed due to poor visibility, making the sighting of signals difficult, so detonator apparatus was used to give an audible warning to the footplate staff that signals were at 'danger' or 'caution'. Falling snow also created hazardous conditions, so the same apparatus was used.

Detonator placing equipment was an important part of the safety arrangements, and there were several types in use. Some machines were worked by the home, starting or advanced starting signal lever, and whenever the signal was at 'danger', so the detonator was in position on the rail. As the signal was pulled off, the detonator was withdrawn. Separate levers were used in some locations and activated when necessary, to comply with the strict instructions in the rule book. At other locations, lineside apparatus was installed, adjacent to which a fog signalman's hut was provided as shelter. Where no placing apparatus was provided detonators were placed upon the rail, with soft metal tabs folded around the rail to clamp the explosive button in position.

Fog signalmen were experienced permanent way men, appointed to specific locations and liable for call out whenever visibility deteriorated, or when other emergency conditions made it necessary. A list of the names and addresses and fogging post allocations was held by both the station master and the signal box for the section, and when called out, the men had to report to the station master before taking up their position. Before appointment as a fog signalman, the individual had to take an examination to test his knowledge of the various rules applying, and his ability to operate the apparatus according to the rules. Poor visibility often occurred during the hours of darkness and where possible, an individual was appointed as the 'caller-up', and his duty was just that - knocking on doors at any hour, to get the other staff out for duty. These individuals were also employed to get enginemen and guards out for normal duty, but this was more of a full time job. Where railway cottages were grouped in an area close to the local station or yard, bells were provided in the cottages of those who were appointed fog signalmen, to be rung in the event that the men were required for duty. Each morning at 7a.m., the Company required that these bells be test rung, and where no means of replying was provided, the railwayman had to report the bell in order to the signalman, before taking up his normal duties. Where warning bells were provided, the services of a 'caller-up' were not required.

The distant signal was the most important one of all, and these were often located some distance from the signal cabin. Whilst the job of the fog signalman was a vitally important one, there can be few more thankless tasks than attending a distant signal, in the middle of nowhere for hours on end and in the middle of the night, repetitively replacing exploded detonators.

The exploding detonator was to attract the attention of the footplate crew, and they were required to reduce speed as quickly as possible and to be able to stop their train immediately as required. The location of signals was known by the drivers, and the detonator at the distant signal indicated the home signal was at 'danger'.

Each fog signalman was provided with a lamp, a red, yellow and green flag and a minumum of 36 detonators, but more where traffic was heavy during the likely period of duty. The fog signalman would stand a short distance behind the detonator placement, and be ready to exhibit the appropriate hand flag signal to the driver of the train. When the signal was 'clear', he had to exhibit a green flag to the driver as he passed.

At some locations, it was necessary for signal indicators to be provided which repeated the position of the signals which may have been out of sight of the fog signalman, and at all times when the signals were 'on', a detonator had to be in position on the rail.

A detonator was kept in position in each machine on the trackside, and as the lineman or ganger walked his length, he was responsible for checking the equipment was in working order and the detonator was in position. In addition, the person responsible for maintaining the signal lamps also checked the equipment.

Snowstorms could, of course, bring particularly hazardous conditions to the line, obliterating the signal arms very quickly. In such conditions, the faithful fog signalman also had to ensure that these were cleaned and visible to approaching trains.

A thankless duty maybe, but one which ensured the safe passage of trains, and the safety of many millions of passengers.

Plate 88 This machine enables the fog signalman to place detonators on the running line without crossing the intervening lines, and at the commencement of duty, it was tested to ensure that it was in working order. The detonator, seen here ready to be drawn along the channel under the intervening lines, was wound until it was in position on the appropriate line. This unusual piece of lineside equipment wouldn't look amiss on model layouts - modellers note!

G. Waite Collection

Plate 89 This and the next plate illustrate Clayton's 'Improved Patent Fog-Signalling Apparatus', which was installed at Derby South Junction. Again, there is much material here for the railway modeller. The lever apparatus here is some 40yds. behind the detonator placing machine, and the signals and normal point or signal type rodding, link the two. The hut was hinged and, when not in use was tilted forward, to cover the coke brazier and rest between the two short posts and upon the bar. The signalman is holding his lamp, detonator container and flags, in what was clearly a demonstration photograph. Another point of interest for the modeller is the raised wooden channelling which is carrying cabling. The lever frame was worked in three positions, the first being 'detonator on line', the second 'clear of line' position, and the third when the gripping jaw was firmly in the magazine. When returned to the first position, it gripped a fresh detonator to place on the line, and was as near to an automatic machine as was at that time possible. These pictures were taken in July 1926. In another part of this book, various styles of signal have been included, the gantry shown here being of Midland origin. Note the straight vertical bands on the distant signals.

G. Waite Collection

Plate 90 The other end of the Clayton machine, placed immediately beneath the signal gantry shown in the previous plate. The detonator is shown resting in position on the rail, whilst the cover and lock to the left are temporarily removed.

G. Waite Collection

Wartime - The War Effort

The years 1939-45 were dark ones in the LMS era, and a period when the railways played a vital role in the history of the nation.

The LMS Board of Directors were superseded by the Government on 1st September 1939, under an order issued in accordance with the provisions of the Emergency Powers (Defence) Act 1939. Peacetime conditions quickly gave way to wartime considerations, and the Minister of Transport appointed the Railway Executive Committee as his agents to control all operational matters.

The Ministry of War Transport was formed in 1941 to work in close liaison with the Railway Executive Committee, and the two posts of Chairman were amalgamated to give smooth communication. Regular meetings of both organizations took place, and frequent conferences to review operational matters were attended by various other committees of railway officers and advisers.

However, war preparations actually commenced in 1937, when the War Office asked the LMS to design a medium tank, a prototype subsequently being built at Crewe Works. This was not suitable, with the military authorities deciding that a lighter and cheaper vehicle was needed. Further design work took place, and from the resultant prototype, the 'Covenanter' was put into production. A total of 1,771 of these was built by a group of companies under the direction of LMS staff, of which 161 were built at Crewe Locomotive Works.

Horwich Works built '481 Cruiser', 'Matilda' and 'Centaur' type tanks, and in addition supplied hundreds of thousands of spares to keep the machines in action. These included clutches, driveshafts and turret rings, which were produced and supplied to the other railway company workshops.

By late 1938, aircraft production was in hand, under the strictest security arrangements. Aircraft wings for 'Hurricanes' and the later 'Typhoons' and 'Tempests' were constructed in several LMS works, with around 4,000 pairs of wings in total being made for the war effort.

Once the war was under way, repairs became vitally important, and damaged aircraft in parts were delivered for attention in four main types, viz: 'Hampden', 'Lancaster' and 'Whitley' bombers, and 'Spitfires'. Barassie Works was responsible for repairs to 'Spitfires', and had the unique distinction of having a runway laid alongside the shop so that when repairs were completed, machines could be flown away.

Other items produced for the war effort included bridge floats for the Navy, 500 carriages for 25 pounder field guns, 60,000 sets of wooden parts for rifles for the Army, thousands of ring and aperture sights for the Royal Air Force, pontoons, bridge sections, bailey bridges, gliders, collapsible assault landing craft and conversions to make armoured vehicles out of tradesmen's road vehicles, to say nothing of ammunition supplies. Also supplied were some 15,000 250 pound bomb casings, 88,500 25 pound shells, 600,000 shell forgings and over six million 20mm. cannon shells, which were manufactured in addition to work on fifteen million more cannon shell cases. This was no mean effort on the part of the LMS and its staff who, remember, also had to cope with maintenance of the railway lines and the equipment.

Railway and road vehicles were added to the war effort, including tankers for the movement of aircraft fuel from rail tankers to the aircraft, and lorries for carrying pipes to sites where new oil lines were being installed. Goods wagons were specially adapted for carrying bombs, and the LMS ran more than 600 bomb specials with an aggregate load of 300,000 tons.

The movement of troops, and the evacuation of families from built-up conurbations to less vulnerable areas, went on throughout the war, with more and more demands being made on both men and equipment.

In addition to all the direct support, the LMS employees also took part in Home Guard protection duties, enlisted for aircraft observer duties, and manned volunteer shifts in makeshift factories to produce specialist components. These spare time activities were undertaken when they were not engaged in making good the effects of bomb damage on their homes, or engaged in their regular work.

LMS hotels were requisitioned to serve as military hospitals, and even the famous Gleneagles Hotel played a major role in this respect.

D-Day, on 6th June 1944, witnessed an offensive in an attempt to finish hostilities. More troop and bomb trains ran, and more vehicle and gun equipment, stores and rations were carried to airfields and ports in 9,769 trains in a three week period, with 3,636 in one week, all to support the move across the channel. One week later, the first flying bomb fell on London, and within a ten week period no fewer than 126 fell on LMS property.

Finance was a major factor throughout the war years, with the Government paying out more than £43 million annually to the four main line companies and the London Passenger Transport Board. The railways, however, had to pay net revenue to the Government, that is, after operating costs had been met. The cost of repairing damage was met from a special scheme set up for public utility undertakings, and once the damage occurred, the work of restoration proceeded immediately.

The end of hostilities brought a welcome breathing space for the railways. Track maintenance had been carried out through necessity, rather than as a means of upgrading stretches of track to permit higher speeds, and locomotives had only been built in small numbers, including the streamlined 'Coronation' class Pacifics during the war period, but the former glorious liveries were no longer applied and drab black was the order of the day. Females had augmented the male staff, and had taken over cleaning and routine maintenance duties, which were hardly suited to their abilities. They had also driven delivery lorries and performed a host of duties in offices, goods depots and stations, as replacement for their menfolk who had been drafted either into the services, or to manufacturing tasks in the workshops.

An unsung part of the LMS staff contribution to the war effort was the voluntary contribution made to various funds. Some £171,000 was raised for the Red Cross 'Penny-a-week Fund', £55,000 for the 'Comforts Fund' for LMS prisoners of war, and more than 1,000 savings groups invested in the War Savings Movement, a total exceeding £489,000.

Lord Stamp, who was Chairman and President of the LMS,

Plate 91 Steel helmets for a locomotive crew, just two of the 669,500 issued to railway employees under the A R P arrangements. To achieve as near black out conditions as possible, the waterproof sheet remains in position between engine and tender, to shield the fireglow from enemy aircraft. Chiefly a measure for night-time work, the covers were left in position. *Duchess of Buccleuch* is pictured carrying yellow shaded red numerals.

V. R. Anderson Collection

was appointed Economic Adviser to the Government and Director of the Bank of England, and his was an untimely death in April 1941, as a result of enemy action. This was a sad loss, so early in the war.

From the cessation of the war in 1945, the LMS had but two and a half years to get things back to normal, before the nationalization of the railways took away its specific identity, but it flourished as one, if not the major, influence on the early years of the new British Railways.

Plate 94 Sandbag protection, for the buildings at Watford Junction Station, in October 1939. Similar protective measures were taken up and down the country, not only on railway property, but also on other property. The chocolate machine is still selling bars for 1d.

British Railways

Plate 95 The LMS converted four dozen goods wagons into twelve armoured trains, and here two such trains are seen outside Derby Works ready for active service, on 5th July 1940. The three plank wagons have axlebox protectors, a coat of paint but little else, whilst the end vehicles have a steel-plated superstructure, a 20mm. gun, and side flaps, which could be lowered inwards as supports for rifles. Food and ammunition supplies were carried on the three plank wagons.

British Railways

Plate 92 (left upper) Huge areas of glass extended over the main termini, and one of the early war tasks was to remove each pane. Here, a gang of men are stripping the roof over Euston Station on 18th July 1940. This was for the benefit of the travelling passengers, before there was any chance of 'Gerry' removing it in a more spectacular manner.

British Railways

Plate 93 (left lower) Southend, on 2nd June 1940, where families are gathered to see their children off to safer places. The vast majority of children had been evacuated in September 1939, but others followed later. School assembly points were used before the movement to the stations, and in all, the first four days of September saw 1,450 special trains carrying half a million children, and supervising adults had been provided by the LMS. Each child wore three labels, and was provided with a gas mask, food supplies and a change of clothing. Destinations were far afield and, for many, new friendships were cast which, even to this day, have withstood the test of time. Small children had mothers to accompany them, but the older ones must have wondered just what was in store for them, leaving home for the very first time. One of the biggest and most speediest evacuations was the removal of the LMS Headquarters, from Euston House to 'The Grove', which was a large country house at Watford, in Hertfordshire. The Company had taken over the property in the spring of 1939, and converted it into office accommodation in readiness for possible war conditions. The move commenced on 1st September, and was completed before 11a.m. on 3rd September, the day when war was declared. Storage of food supplies also became an evacuation job, and the LMS assisted in moving large quantities from the London area to rural areas, where suitable storage accommodation was available.

British Railways

Plate 96 A photograph of troops being drilled on the most unlikely of 'barrack squares', the sidings at Willesden, on 12th December 1939. Full battledress is the order of the day, with steel helmets, rifles and packs indicating that Willesden sidings were some sort of a reception centre for volunteers. After basic drill, kitting out and documentation, the new recruits could then have moved on to army units. Prior to war breaking out, preparations had begun to train railway personnel for army duties, and a number of military units were established. Longmoor Military Camp, in Hampshire, was the annual training centre for the officers and men in the Supplementary Reserve Transportation Units of the Corps of Royal Engineers, and the Royal Corps of Signals. The LMS provided one Railway Workshop Company and a (line of communication) Signal Company, and also fathered the formation of a docks unit, which in addition to railwaymen, was also open to dock employees. 'Railway troops' were given leave to attend the annual summer camps, and their training included the building of station platforms from sleepers and rail, and the re-equipment of the workshops of the Longmoor Military Railway. The Resident Mechanical Engineer at the LMS locomotive shops at Bow in East London was the enlistment officer for LMS employees wishing to join the Supplementary Reserve. A bounty of between £6 and £15 was paid to each man, dependent upon the trade in which he enlisted, related, of course, to his normal employment with the Company. Work periods were generally during the mornings, and recreational activities, including sports, rifle shooting etc. occupied the fifteen day training period.

British Railways

Plate 97 An LMS vestibule carriage, in use as an orderly room at Willesden on 12th December 1939, with an officer, sergeant and private, all unimpressed by the luxury of an LMS vehicle. The side couches have been moved in to replace the standard seating. The pattern of the cloth could date the stock as LMS period I, from 1923 to 1928/9.

British Railways

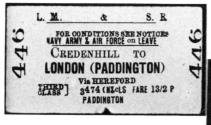

Plate 98 Mobile canteens played an important role in keeping the workers at their jobs by taking food to them. This Commer 15 cwt. chassis was part of Wolverton Order No. 4364, built around 1940/1. This vehicle is numbered in the service section of the fleet.

British Railways

Plate 99 A converted container, photographed aboard an ex-LNWR carriage truck, while serving as Mobile Canteen No. 1. The steps and cornerpieces, as well as the interior of the canteen, are painted white, to aid visibility in hours of darkness. This container canteen was also photographed on the back of a lorry and a horse dray, no doubt an exercise aimed at assessing its suitability for service in different locations.

British Railways

Plate 100 A heavily-loaded train, pictured whilst in the process of disgorging civilians and troops. Those who have served in the forces need no reminder that the kitbags carried everything, even down to the 'little housewife', which was a sewing kit, for those who never had the privilege. Airmen, soldiers and sailors in uniform were always moving hither and thither between units, and once on the train, legs were up and heads were down in order to catch up on much needed sleep.

British Railways

Plate 101 (right) Unparalleled activity was the keynote during the war years, and this extended to a nationwide salvage campaign. Tickets, envelopes, paper, textiles, ropes, bottles, bones, straw and even paper fasteners were collected for recycling into usable materials. Every possible form of salvage which was considered to have a second life was saved and collected, and at every station, garage, depot, workshop and office, both on and off the railways, the staff were galvanized into collecting salvage. The scheme was of such national importance that salvage officers and leaders were appointed to intensify local collection, and publicity schemes by travelling exhibitions, posters and film shows were used to keep interest aroused. Salvage bins were provided, and regular collections were made to transfer the materials to central points. The vast bulk of salvage was carried by the railways, and staff are seen here loading sacks into an appropriately labelled van. For the railway modeller, the LMS style handtruck and a former L&NWR flat trolley are of interest, but note also the chalk writing on the van side.

G. Foxley Collection

Plate 102 A photograph, taken on 12th December 1940, showing war damage at the south end of Sheffield (Midland) Station and the major damage done to the properties which overlooked this important station. The signal box has suffered severe blast damage, and the greater part of the boarding requires replacement. If the smoke is to be believed, then the stove in the cabin is still burning, and of note is the buffer stop and rails, which have been painted white. Signal cabins were stoutly constructed, but because of the height and large areas of boarding or glass, they were particularly susceptible to blast damage, so cellophane or hessian coverings were applied to many signal box windows.

British Railways

Plate 103 The end of platform 5, pictured on the same day, where signal engineers are working to build up a replacement lever frame for installation in the south station box.

British Railways

Plate 104 Particularly badly damaged was St. Pancras Station, with three direct hits occurring within a month in late 1940, one of which caused a five day closure. If the glass had not already been removed, then casualties could have been much worse. On 10th May 1941, the station was hit again and, on this occasion, remained closed for a week whilst major repairs were completed. This scene of devastation is on the departure side, close to the concourse area.

British Railways

Plate 105 The cratered area is highlighted by the new platform work, newly-ballasted track and the cellar replacement work taking place below the ground level. St. Pancras is once again a hive of activity, although the station is not yet back to normal.

British Railways

Plate 106 Damaged steelwork, in the great arch yawning above the St. Pancras platform area, on 15th October 1940. Steel-helmeted staff are engaged in tidying up operations, whilst huge piles of goods and mailbags wait to continue their journey. In the right foreground are one or two names to conjour with, these being Eldorado Ice Cream Co. Ltd. and Lyons Ice Cream, pictured on waiting containers, whilst a crate of Grenson Shoes lies on the opposite side of the roadway. A mailbag train of trolleys is headed by a Lansing 'Imp' petrol tractor.

British Railways

Plate 107 St. Pancras Station, on 20th September 1943, and an ambulance train has just arrived with casualties for a fleet of ambulances and ambulance buses, waiting to take them either to their homes or hospitals.

British Railways

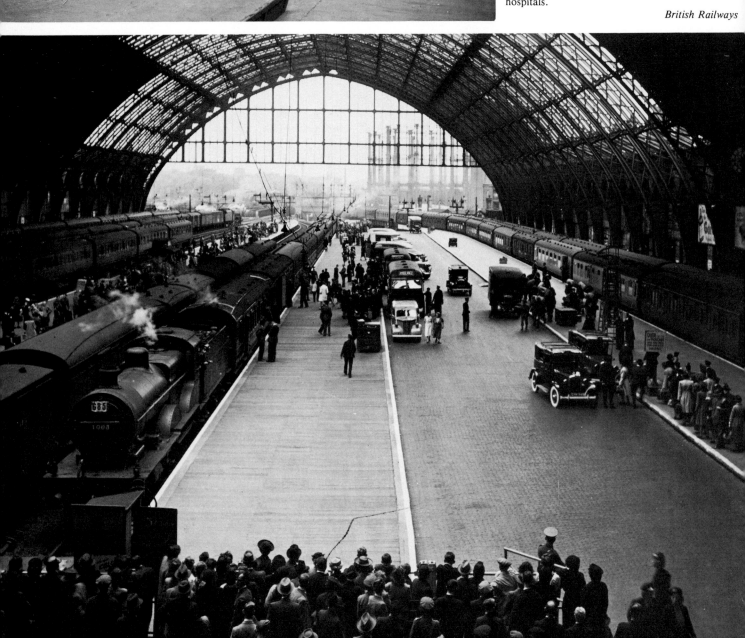

Plate 108 Aircraft wing sections under repair in specially constructed jigs, in Derby Carriage Works. When compared with today's aircraft, these are mere minnows.

British Railways

Plate 109 Wing sections and fusilages pictured whilst under repair, with some requiring greater attention than others.

British Railways

Plate 110 Rather more attention on the wings in this view, with the outer skin being peeled right back in some instances. Only the roof lights are open to the natural light.

British Railways

Plate 111 What must rank as 'the picture' of an aeroplane, pictured when the gentleman has just stepped back after applying stencilled lettering 'LMSR/R/CRAF' in black. The type doesn't really matter.

British Railways

Plate 112   The staff canteen at the Derby Carriage & Wagon Works during wartime years, with the stage being occupied by one of the all-time orchestral greats, Joe Loss and his orchestra. The occasion was a B B C broadcast, on 20th August 1943. Facilities 'somewhere in England' were often used for broadcasting and entertaining purposes, and on such occasions in works canteens, the railway staff were able to attend both lunchtime and evening performances.

National Railway Museum

Plate 113   A full house for Joe Loss with a sea of faces all engrossed in the entertainment being provided. These two photographs also provide useful details of the construction of the building.

National Railway Museum

Plate 114   A wartime closure handbill for this North Scotland branch line. The line opened in 1903 as part of the Highland Railway system.

Author's Collection

Plate 115   The LMS continued to operate its motor vehicle fleet, and this 2 ton Dennis is shown in wartime livery, with white markings added to the crimson livery. The two large cylinders at the side of the engine, were a wartime fuel economy measure which allowed the vehicle to run on producer gas instead of petrol, as large quantities of this were required to keep the aircraft flying. One headlight has a mask fitted, to direct such light as was available on to the road.

British Railways

LMS

B. 23630

Closing
OF
WICK AND LYBSTER BRANCH

The London Midland and Scottish Railway Company intimate that the Wick and Lybster Branch Railway will be closed for the conveyance of traffic by rail after the finish of work on **Saturday, 1st April, 1944.**

On and from Monday, 3rd April, passengers will not be booked for rail conveyance to or from :—

THRUMSTER	ROSTER ROAD
WELSH'S CROSSING	OCCUMSTER
ULBSTER	PARKSIDE
MID CLYTH	LYBSTER

There is a convenient 'bus service serving the area, to which passengers are referred.

Passenger train parcels, newspapers, and perishable passenger train traffic, such as fish, etc., will be conveyed between Wick and the stations on the Branch by road motor vehicle working from and to Wick Station.

Freight Train traffic will also be conveyed between Wick and the Branch Line Stations in either direction by road motor vehicle working from and to Wick Station.

The existing arrangements at Lybster regarding the collection and delivery of traffic, that is, between the station and the traders' premises, will continue.

MALCOLM SPEIR,
Chief Officer for Scotland.

E.R.O. 53302

L—21/3/44—No. 1—McCorquodale, Glasgow

Plate 116 Signal cabin No. 1 at Watford, on 16th October 1939, with the signalman trying out the indoor air raid shelter provided for his safety. On the shelf are four boxes of Duplex fog signals - detonators - and a box lettered for 'gloves & mat'.

British Railways

Plate 117 Victory Day decorations adorn the outside of Euston Station on 8th June 1945, and after all that had occupied the dark days since 1939, this was a time for celebrations. The fifth and seventh clusters of flags from the left were above banners bearing the LMS crest. Servicemen walking into the station would not be alone in welcoming final victory and the end of the war.

British Railways

LMS Bric-à-Brac

Literally anything falls into this section, through having the Company's initials embossed, engraved, or painted on to it. Many hundreds of thousands of items were in existence, and these are but a few examples which have survived.

Plate 118 A dining car attendant's button. Whilst all staff uniforms had buttons with the LMS crest embossed thereon, the dining car staff were singled out for special treatment as they were, after all, considered a prestigious part of the Company's service, and were attired in either dinner waistcoat or dinner jacket and bow tie.

G. Foxley Collection

Plate 119 A small paraffin burner, used by the locomotive lighting-up gangs. Locomotives arriving on shed would either be kept in steam for a quick turnround, or if not rostered for a day or two or when undergoing regular examination, the fire would be dropped. When rostered for a turn, the fire would be relaid, and the shed staff carried one of these burners in flame to set the fire burning. Many thousands were in use, and as with most of the Company's property, the LMS letters were prominently embossed.

Author's Collection

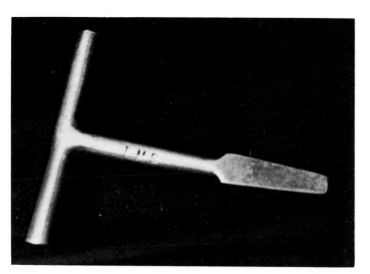

Plate 120 Have you ever wondered what key was used to lock carriage doors? Well, this is the one.

G. Foxley Collection

Plate 121 Everything which could possibly be labelled with the Company's initials carried them. This ashtray is one example, and is of the type used in carriage toilets. The interlaced letters were the earlier style used, with later styles utilizing the three simple matching letters.

G. Foxley Collection

Plate 123 (above) Blankets for the sleeping carriages, and rugs, which were available for hire from rug and pillow trucks on platforms, had the LMS lettering incorporated in the patterns. This blanket is coloured brown on cream.

G. Foxley Collection

Plate 122 (top left) Everything owned by the Company was lettered, even this privately-made clock. The LMS had a clock and watch department at its Manchester (Osborne Street) Depot, with repairs to both passengers' and goods guards' watches being carried out, as well as repairs to clocks for the stations and depots in the Manchester area.

Author's Collection

Plate 124 (left) This is a small carpet from a first class saloon, and is predominantly green base with cream, brown and black in the design.

G. Foxley Collection

Plate 126 (bottom right) A label from a railway issue raincoat handed out at Normanton, but unlike the next photograph, the label was easily removed.

G. Foxley Collection

Plate 127 (bottom centre) Heavy overcoats were supplied to all but the works and office staff, and all carried a pasted-in label of the type shown here, although this was for the Midland Division. Again, the item was issued from Normanton.

G. Foxley Collection

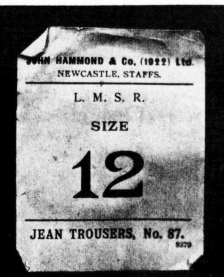

Plate 125 (above) A label of a commercial supplier of uniform items to the Company, in this instance trousers, and 'jeans' at that!

G. Foxley Collection

Poster Publicity

Punctual train services were the constant aim of the Company, and records were kept to monitor timekeeping of public services. There were periods when timekeeping reached the dizzy level of 90 per cent for trains 'punctual to within five minutes of scheduled times', and for odd weeks, the figure went up to more than 96 per cent. The term 'within five minutes' obviously covered a multitude of minor operating impediments. The early years after the Grouping had seen similar figures around the 70 per cent mark and through all-round effort, including improved track standards and more powerful locomotives, these punctuality figures had shown improvement. By 1931, the LMS could point to more than 6,000 services which had had timings accelerated, and the punctuality improvements were therefore a good achievement. Important freight trains were also measured, and 71 per cent were punctual or within thirty minutes of booked time.

Clean and healthy carriages were the unending aim, and the principal passenger services were allocated the new rolling stock as it came into service. This was indeed one of the principal points referred to by LMS sales staff, particularly on Anglo-Scottish services where competition from the LNER existed. Spitting was prohibited, with identifiable offenders being prosecuted.

Good meals nicely served in comfortable dining cars of first class appointment, along with the attraction of a drink with a meal. With the Company's involvement in its hotel chain, it was well-placed to offer the same standard of meals and service in its 'mobile restaurants'.

Civility and attention to a passenger's every need was an oft-repeated cliché, and the Company's view was that a well-satisfied passenger would be disposed to recommend the LMS to his friends, and this was translated into increased revenue.

Plate 129
What else can one say?
This poster was issued immediately after the Grouping, as a reassurance to the public who were faced with this huge new conglomerate, and human nature is no different even today.

Author's Collection

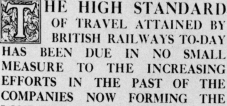

STILL BETTER SERVICE

THE HIGH STANDARD OF TRAVEL ATTAINED BY BRITISH RAILWAYS TO-DAY HAS BEEN DUE IN NO SMALL MEASURE TO THE INCREASING EFFORTS IN THE PAST OF THE COMPANIES NOW FORMING THE LONDON MIDLAND AND SCOTTISH—THE LARGEST RAILWAY IN BRITAIN.

IT WILL BE THE CONSTANT AIM OF THE MANAGEMENT FURTHER TO IMPROVE THIS STANDARD SO THAT

PUNCTUAL TRAIN SERVICES,
CLEAN & HEALTHY CARRIAGES,
GOOD MEALS NICELY SERVED,
CIVILITY & ATTENTION,

WILL BE KNOWN AS THE DISTINGUISHING CHARACTERISTICS
OF THE

LONDON MIDLAND AND SCOTTISH RAILWAY

COMPRISING THE
LONDON & NORTH WESTERN; MIDLAND;
LANCASHIRE & YORKSHIRE;
NORTH STAFFORDSHIRE; FURNESS;
CALEDONIAN; GLASGOW & SOUTH WESTERN,
AND HIGHLAND RAILWAYS

January 1923

ARTHUR WATSON,
GENERAL MANAGER

Plate 130 The 1925 Blackpool Trade and Commerce Procession attracted this entry from the LMS and it later gained first prize, with the certificate attached to the dray and the rosettes worn by the horse and the leading drayman. The dray carries a large display of the pictorial painting series commissioned by the LMS from eminent Royal Academy artists, and the coaching stock is still in L&YR livery. Similar dray displays featured in parades and horse shows throughout the railway territory, and such was the high standard of presentation achieved by the carting and horse staff, that the Company's entries were rarely out of the honours.

National Railway Museum

Plate 131 This decorated dray is being used to advertise holidays by the LMS, while railway staff hand out brochures to the public in Nottingham. The horse has been well turned out, complete with white ear-muffs.

Author's Collection

FETTES COLLEGE
By NORMAN WILKINSON P.R.I.

Fettes College, Edinburgh, so named after its Founder, Sir William Fettes, Bart. who was twice Lord Provost of the City, was opened in 1870 with Dr. Alexander Potts, the famous Classical Scholar of his day, as Headmaster. The architect of this fine building was David Bryce, R.S.A. and the beautiful grounds owe much for their design to the School's first Chairman of Governors, Lord Justice-General John Inglis of Glencorse. The College stands on commanding ground with a glorious view of Arthur's Seat, the Castle Rock and the many buildings and steeples of the old town silhouetted against the sky. The School's Motto is INDUSTRIA.

FAMOUS PUBLIC SCHOOLS ON THE LMS

Plate 132 The Fettes College was one of a series of posters featuring famous public schools on the LMS, which included Oundle and Sedbergh Schools in the single royal size, and those at Harrow and Rugby in the larger double royal size. They were produced from original paintings by Norman Wilkinson, PRI, and the LMS crest was also reproduced in full colour.
Author's Collection

Plate 133 A specific event poster for 1929, printed in blue and red to catch the eye. Between 1st January and 31st December 1929, railway-owned and operated horse stock increased from 18,510 to 19,352, with the LMS share being 9,111 and 9,431 at the commencement and end of year respectively. The majority of these were of the heavy breeds, Clydesdale, Shires and Suffolk Punch, but for van work, lighter animals were used. The LMS was a big supporter of horse shows, parades and special events, and encouraged carters to prepare and exhibit those animals in their care, and with a great measure of success. LMS horses often took the major prizes, and the real benefits came from the loving care lavished on the animals, the ever faithful horses.

Author's Collection

Plate 134 There was a wide range of both single and double royal posters, featuring holiday locations and places of interest to remind the railway public and create sufficient interest to get them into travelling on the railway to see them. This North Wales example is from a series issued in 1938/9. A wide range of posters was prepared principally for station billboards and display in travel agent and railway enquiry offices, including a series on British industries, castles, docks and famous cities, to mention but a few.

Author's Collection

Seat Reservations

Plate 135 Three carriage labels, each 5in. x 6in., and printed in red.

Author's Collection

DOLBADARN CASTLE, LLANBERIS

NORTH WALES for HOLIDAYS

LONDON, MIDLAND AND SCOTTISH RAILWAY.

Identification of reserved seats was made easier for the passenger when, in the spring of 1934, the LMS introduced distinctive letter markings for carriages. At Euston and other termini, large letter boards were suspended from wires running above the platforms, thus enabling the passenger to move to the carriage with a corresponding identification label. Whilst these sample labels are red on white, the early markings were black on yellow. Seat reservation tickets were, thereafter, marked with the appropriate coach letter and seat number and, as a further aid for passengers, reserved seat attendants on the platform were distinguished by the distinctive yellow armlets and cap-bands that they wore.

Plate 136 Reserved labels were placed in the carriages to correspond with the ticket given to the passenger, and these are two of the many types issued. The compartment sticker is green, whilst the 'all seats' one is bright red.

Author's Collection

L. M. S.
RESERVED COMPARTMENT
E.R.O. 48838.
FROM
TO
NAME
Train
Date
Joining at
Station Master.

LMS
ALL SEATS RESERVED
PASSENGERS JOIN AT
E.R.O. 48842
O.P. 2

No. 19

LMS
ONE SEAT RESERVED
in
1st CLASS DINING CAR

Passengers when proceeding to the Dining Car are requested to take their Railway Tickets with them.

Passengers are also desired to leave the Car as soon as the meal is finished, in order that the Attendants may serve another meal.

SECOND SITTING

Plate 137 A specially-built trolley for storage of the train indication boards referred to in the previous plate, seen in use at Euston. The livery appears to be Crimson Lake, with white reference numbers and gold LMS reservations lettering.

Author's Collection

RESERVED
SEATS
1/-
FROM
Terminal Stations

Postcards

Postcards, playing cards, jigsaws and books of trains were all published by the LMS, with more than a hint that they were intended for the schoolboy fraternity.

Postcards were produced both in full colour and in black and white, with sepia-toned ones also available. Subjects covered included locomotives, with descriptions and data on the reverse, the Company's steamships, again with related data on the back, a considerable number of LMS hotel cards, and a number of cards best described as 'miscellaneous subjects'.

Some of the hotel cards were used as acknowledgement cards by the Company Registrar operating from the Secretary's Office at Euston, in repect of a shareholder's change of address or dividend request instructions. Both were a practical way of advertising the Company hotels.

Several cards depicting LMS holiday caravans were available, and from the messages on some, the customers using them were well satisfied.

Jigsaws and books of trains were intended for the younger generation, particularly for those who were on long journeys, and these were available from station bookstalls or by post. The jigsaws were 5½in. x 3in., and those of the 'Royal Scot' class engine were priced at 6d each.

Books of trains, which included locomotives of the LMS past and present, were priced at 3s 6d each, this being a princely sum in pre-war days. Also,

at 1s 0d, *Modern Locomotives of the LMS*, which was published by the Locomotive Publishing Co. Ltd., had the full backing of the LMS, and was produced to normal book standards.

One colour postcard, with an LMS furniture removal container on a Karrier lorry, was given away with the *LMS Magazine* to advertise this service. An illustration of this postcard can be found as *Plate 232* in the first volume of *LMS Miscellany*.

Plate 138 Some LMS postcard issues, showing the Welcombe Hotel card in use prior to the official opening in 1931, with the reverse side being used to acknowledge dividend instructions. The erecting shop card was the only one featuring this type of subject, although there were engine cards as can be seen in the next plate. The *T S S Duke of Lancaster* is a rather superb colour card, one of several issued featuring the Company's ships.

B. Hilton Collection

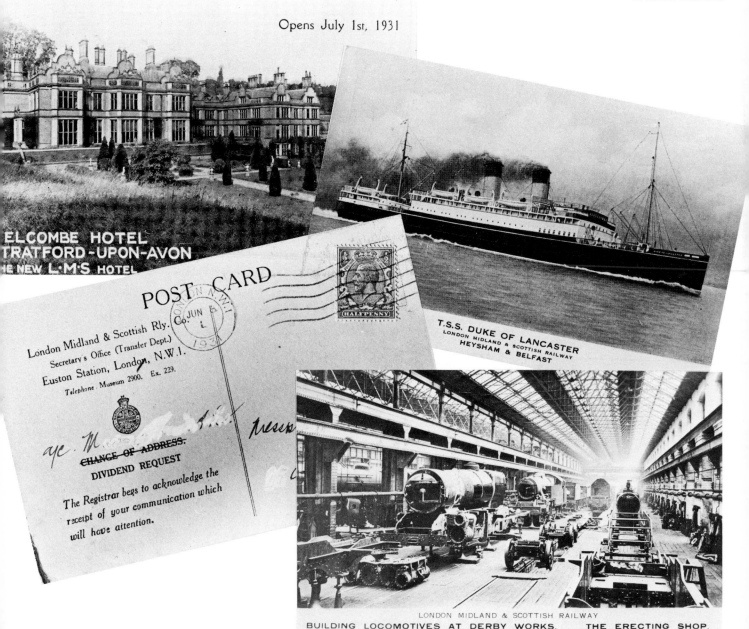

Plate 139 The post-war set of engine cards, complete with the envelope in which they were sold, showing locomotives in the 1946 black livery. These cards were popular with children, but as with so many things in the pre-preservation/pre-collecting period, they were soon forgotten and the vast majority no doubt found their way into the dustbin.

LMS PASSENGER TANK LOCOMOTIVE No. 2673 'Class 4'
Designed: C. E. FAIRBURN   Built: 1945

LMS FREIGHT LOCOMOTIVE No. 8111 Class 8
Designed: SIR WILLIAM STANIER, F.R.S.   Built: 1939

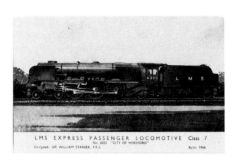

LMS MIXED TRAFFIC LOCOMOTIVE No. 4931 Class 5
Designed: SIR WILLIAM STANIER, F.R.S.   Built: 1946

L M S LOCOMOTIVES IN COLOUR

PRICE 1/6 *Including Purchase Tax*

PRICE 1/6 *Including Purchase Tax*

1 4-6-2 "Coronation" Class
2 4-6-0 Rebuilt "Royal Scot"
3 4-6-0 Mixed Traffic Cl.5
4 2-6-4 Cl.4 Tank
5 2-8-0 Cl.8 Freight
6 2-6-0 Cl.2 Freight

SIX - POSTCARDS - SIX

LMS EXPRESS PASSENGER LOCOMOTIVE Class 7
No. 6253 "CITY OF HEREFORD"
Designed: SIR WILLIAM STANIER, F.R.S.   Built: 1946

LMS FREIGHT LOCOMOTIVE No. 6400 Class 2
Designed: H. G. IVATT   Built: 1946

LMS EXPRESS PASSENGER LOCOMOTIVE Class 6
No. 6133 "THE GREEN HOWARDS"
CONVERTED TO TAPER BOILER BY SIR WILLIAM STANIER, F.R.S. IN 1944

Parcel Stamps

Plate 140 Well over 44 million parcels each weighing less than 2 cwt. were carried annually by the LMS in the early 1930s, and the figure continued to rise each year. Excess luggage items, mails and parcel post added to this total, with total receipts exceeding £5,000,000 sterling each year. Charges were paid and parcel stamps affixed, and these are examples of the ones used. Printed in red on white toilet type tissue and gummed, they were an every day part of the railway scene, and many millions of these were printed in the Company's own printing works.

Plate 141 (below) A prepaid newspaper parcel stamp, valued at three farthings. In the 1860s, W. H. Smith had arranged, with the railway companies, for special rates to apply to newspaper parcels sent across the country to its bookstalls on stations. Again, the special stamps were red on white, this time on a better quality gummed paper, but on the Midland Division, who would expect anything but the best.

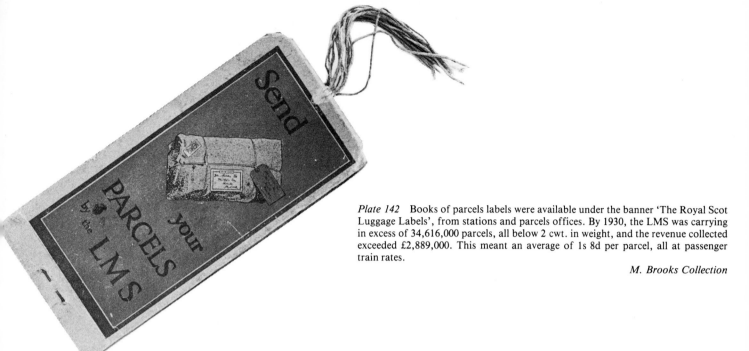

Plate 142 Books of parcels labels were available under the banner 'The Royal Scot Luggage Labels', from stations and parcels offices. By 1930, the LMS was carrying in excess of 34,616,000 parcels, all below 2 cwt. in weight, and the revenue collected exceeded £2,889,000. This meant an average of 1s 8d per parcel, all at passenger train rates.

M. Brooks Collection

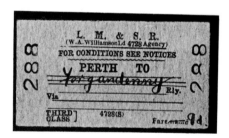

Station Scenes

The railway stations of today and the general atmosphere surrounding them, are in no way the same as those that characterized the steam railway era. This is particularly true of the period to which this book is devoted, 1923 to 1948. The modeller, therefore, has to rely on photographs of the bygone era, and the aim in the following plates is to give an impression of LMS stations, although in turn, some of the scenes have changed little from the pre-group era.

The majority of stations were not of the 'hustle and bustle' nature associated with Crewe or Carlisle, but trains came and went, interspersed with long quiet periods when nothing more than a motor van was emptied, with the boxes and parcels being loaded on to a platform trolley and then trundled along the platform to await the arrival of the appropriate train. As passengers gathered, so the countdown to the train arrival was often heralded by the signal being pulled off and the shout of 'clanger' from the train-spotters, followed by a short period of anxious anticipation. Dependent on the time of day and the train, one would often hear 'would we get a seat without trouble', 'are we in the right place', 'porter, is this the London/Crewe/Bedford train' (a reassuring answer was expected), 'here it

is, it's not too full', 'oh yes plenty of seats'. All anxiety quickly disappeared as an air of satisfaction enveloped the none too sure passenger. The major stations are, of course, the ones which are best remembered by the majority of travellers, but the small country stations were just as important, and what is more, the staff were no less informed than their more pretentious colleagues.

The pride of the line were the men, and their pride was in answering every question from the passenger, including questions from main line connections for 'their' trains, times of arrival in distant places and the best method of sending a parcel or package - and they didn't have to refer to the good book to give the right answer. There was a desire to please, to smile, and to help whenever they could.

To the public, the stations whether they were large or small, were the LMS, for the vast majority of people who experienced the LMS were passengers and not railway enthusiasts or photographers, but I suspect that there have been many people since nationalization who wished they'd taken more of an interest, bought a camera, or just made interesting notes on what happened. For them, the following station pictures will be of interest.

Plate 143   Perth, and a crowded platform waits the arrival of 4-6-0 'Jubilee' No. 5579 *Punjab*. Porters line the platform edge to open doors and as a precaution against passengers being tempted too near the platform edge. Several signs here are of interest, particularly the one indicating the presence of the LNER office, for this was a joint station.

V. R. Anderson Collection

Plate 144   Lightcliffe, between Bradford (Exchange) and Halifax, with former L&YR tank engine No. 10804 pictured on a local passenger service. The station name is painted on the platform seat.

G. Coltas

Plate 145 The summer of 1930 in the Derbyshire Peak District sees an overcast day at Edale Station, on the Hope Valley line between Manchester and Sheffield. There is much to interest the modeller in this picture, including the entrance to the signal cabin which is at the back, the fencing with stout bars, the uncluttered trackwork, the loading gauge, lamps, rolled tarpaulin sheets on the platform awaiting dispatch by the next train to the sheet depot at Trent and, not least, a long line of 'Bolsover' private owner coal wagons in the yard. The three gentlemen in bowler hats are probably area officials from Sheffield.

G. Waite Collection

Plate 146 Trent Station looking south and, as stated in *LMS Miscellany* Volume I, this was a most unusual station, located just over a mile from Long Eaton. The north end was paved with large York stone slabs, and because most staff used cycles to reach the station, a paved path led all the way alongside the track to Long Eaton. To the far left can be seen the inclined track, which crossed over the Nottingham to Trent lines, and led directly to the Toton Marshalling Yard a mile north of Long Eaton Station. This avoiding line was used extensively by coal trains to and from the London area, often with a 'Garratt' at the head of a long line of wagons.

British Railways

Plate 147 Elford was a small country station between Burton-on-Trent and Tamworth, on the main Midland line to Birmingham and Bristol. Elford was one of the smallest of villages, and it was perhaps unusual that it received a station of this size. The low station platform was a relic of the early Midland Railway period, or even the Birmingham & Derby Junction Company which had been absorbed into the Midland in 1844. It remained in use until the late 1950s.

Author's Collection

148 The south end of Leicester Midland Station on 30th December 1925,
~~c~~haracteristically quiet and indicating a Sunday photograph. This is another view which
~~i~~s interest for the modeller, and includes the Midland water-column with lamptop
~~mo~~unted above floor level on a brick and stone plinth, and the standard Midland lamp
~~stan~~dard and the bracket signal. The fish-tail distant has the white band straight across the
~~end~~ of the signal arm, and is painted the same colour as the home arm. The calling on
~~sign~~al is a hammer-head type, covering movements from the middle third track which ran
~~thro~~ugh the length of the station. Trains for the Leicester to Burton service often stood on
~~this~~ centre line, before moving into the platform after the St. Pancras service had left. The
~~door~~way on the left was the way out for excursion traffic, the main stairway being some
~~way~~ back along the platform.

G. Waite Collection

149 Station buildings feature in many photographs, but there are not so many taken
~~of i~~nterior features, and this is sometimes a quite unhelpful situation for the railway
~~mod~~eller. Cast-iron urinals have been available in model form for several years, but some
~~mod~~ellers may wish to model the interior detail of a gentlemen's cloakroom. Here, at the
~~new~~ly-constructed Southend East Station in March 1932, is just one such example. The
~~lam~~pshades remind me of those used in the school I attended during and after the war
~~yea~~rs. The taps on the left of each basin are the normal screw type cold taps, whilst those
~~on t~~he right are the press-to-operate type, designed to conserve hot water.

G. Waite Collection

L. M. & S. R.
FOR CONDITIONS SEE BACK
PASSENGER TICKET BY GOODS TRAIN
5309 Train on ...6- 9- 1956
From CULRAIN
To INVERSHIN
Not available for any other Stations
Fare .... s. .. d

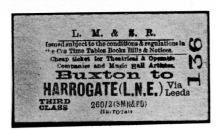

Plate 150 Preston Station, just after lunch on 19th May 1944, showing dark and busy platforms, which were so much a part of the real railway scene and had been virtually unchanged for generations. The concrete-posted compound in the foreground is a recent addition, and is part of the Claims Prevention protection specially provided for parcels traffic. Note the subway access signs and the signal gantry just below the clock. The reference numbers on the left-hand wall are parcel destination codes.

V. R. Anderson Collection

Plate 151 Manchester (Exchange) Station, pictured on 12th September 1941 after considerable restoration following bomb damage. There is much of interest for the modeller, including the cobbled and covered cabway, the arc roof sections which still have evidence of damage and the various platform signs, etc.

V. R. Anderson Collection

Plate 152 Towcester Station, photographed on 30th March 1926, and with every appearance of it being a quiet Sunday morning. Towcester was a junction on the Stratford-upon-Avon & Midland Junction Railway, with three platform faces and services radiating to Stratford, eastwards to Olney, to link up with the former Midland line from Northampton to Bedford, south-west to Banbury, and north to Blisworth and Northampton. Again, a print full of interest for the railway modeller, particularly anyone looking for a prototype location in a country setting, yet a busy and important junction none the less.

G. Waite Collection

Plate 153 This picture is believed to be Bradford-on-Avon, a point to which the Company did not run. This was a goods and parcel receiving office, and passenger tickets were issued valid from either Bath or Bristol. The LMS boards all appear to be new. The Great Western Railway poster-board, on the far side of the LMS office, advertises through express trains between the GWR and the London & North Eastern Railway stations.

British Railways

Plate 154 Not all small termini stations boasting a covered roof were on the GWR, and this view of Bothwell Station, which is south-east of Glasgow, confirms that fact. Built by the Caledonian Railway, the station was at the end of a branch from Fallside, with services coming through from Glasgow Central (Low Level). The water on the right-hand platform would indicate that the glass had been removed from the roof, and note that the poster-boards all carry the lettering LMS. Bothwell was something of an unusual prototype.

A. G. Ellis

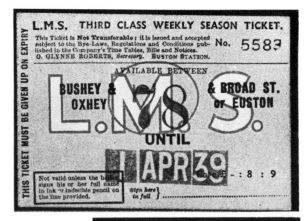

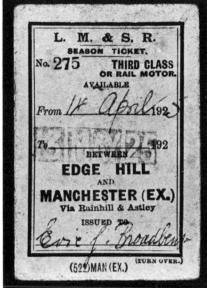

Plate 155 The Doric Arch at the entrance to Euston Station, not basking in summer sunshine but illuminated during the hours of darkness. This was almost testimony to the 'we never close' theme, to which the LMS could justly lay claim.

Author's Collection

Plate 156 The pedestrian subway at Manchester (Victoria), lined with salt-glazed bricks and commercial advertising posters. The LMS poster proclaims a huge success for the weekly season tickets newly introduced in 1926, and sales continued to increase year upon year. Subways were a regular feature at the principal and main line stations.

National Railway Museum

Plate 157 The south end of Bromsgrove Station, round about the 1927/8 period, showing the rather splendid gantry built by the Midland Railway, which was replaced a week or so after this photograph was taken. There are several features of interest to modellers, not least the crossover with slips linking four tracks, and the platform edging bricks. Note too the straight fencing, and leading from this the spur line, which has no buffer stop but may well have had a track stop.

C. Gilbert

Plate 158 The road overbridge at Hendon, pictured in March 1925, showing the part not often seen in photographs of the railway scene. Nevertheless, this was an important part, and there were many thousands of similar roadways across the railway. The young boy engrossed in the photographer's actions gives a good illustration of why the walls to the roadway were around 7ft. in height, the idea being that young boys couldn't climb them, though many did. The rather splendid example of the rear of a tall Midland bracket signal and the straight fencing may help the modeller.

G. Waite Collection

78 HENDON MAR 25 1925

Plate 159 A pedestrian underpass or subway at Macclesfield, a good example of a structure which was often found in towns and cities along the route of the railway. This view, taken in 1932, shows a bricked rather than cobbled walkway. There were hundreds of these scattered around the system, and many were within the station area.

G. Waite Collection

Plate 160 Leeds (Wellington) Station frontage, with artwork superimposed over the original print intended to show a scheme for improving the appearance of the street entrance, which had been virtually unchanged since the station was built in 1846. In the event, the LMS did not proceed with the scheme shown. Few people using this station could have known that all the platforms were constructed on girders which spanned the River Aire. The dark building to the left is the old LMS-owned Queen's Hotel, which was later demolished in 1935 to make way for the new 'Queen's' which, at the time, was considered to be the most modern hotel in Europe.

G. Waite Collection

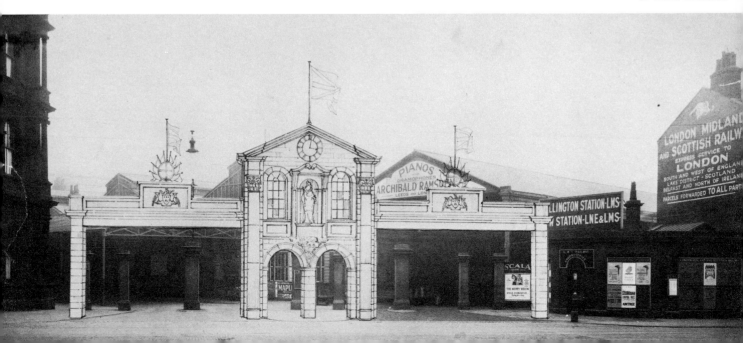

Plates 161 & 162 Derby (Midland) Station, on 17th September 1925, displaying a newly installed chronometer with advertising panels. It can hardly be described as a station clock, rather more a time indicator. When comparing the two plates, it is obvious that the hour panel changes during the hour. If the hour panel were to change every minute in line with the minute panel for a full twelve hour sequence, 720 hour panels would be required. The timepiece cabinet does not appear sufficiently large to take this number of panels in the hours section alone, so it is probable, therefore, that there were sixty hour panels with five changes of panel each hour. This was undoubtedly a new type of timepiece which produced advertising revenue. Electric Advertising Clocks Ltd. of Beak Street, London are shown as advertising agents on behalf of the LMS.

G. Waite Collection

Plate 163 An unusual view of St. Pancras Station looking over Midland Road. The great arch was built in 1867 using more than 9,000 tons of iron supplied by the Butterley Company and 17,000 squares of glass, covering 2½ acres. It is 105ft. above rail level, 240ft. wide and 690ft. long, and more than 6,000 men were employed in constructing the station. Quite apart from the area normally seen by those using the trains, were three floors beneath the platforms which were let out to the Burton brewers, Bass, Ratcliff & Gretton Ltd. Hydraulic hoists or lifts were provided between floors, and this ale store served all parts of London with daily deliveries of ale and beer. The LMS Hotels Department also used a part of these cellars for an extensive wine and spirit store. In this 1928 view, the board above the archway No. 10 carries the faint name of 'Frank Mason, Advertising Contractor', whilst the other archways permit access to the area beneath the station, although those in the foreground could well be stable accommodation for the Company's horses.

G. Waite Collection

Plate 164 In the bowels of St. Pancras Station, a variety of trades was carried on, as well as it being a storage place for ale and spirits. This workshop is quite well equipped to deal with general repair requirements.

G. Waite Collection

Telegraph and Telephone Communications

The Company had its own internal facilities for both telegraphic and telephonic communication between stations and office centres. Messages relating to things such as operational matters and delays to trains etc. were telegraphed along the routes, and frequently the messages received, stating that delays would occur, were exhibited in the window of the telegraph office fronting the station platform. Urgent messages reporting accidents or incidents had priority.

Travelling train attendants and ticket collectors carried a supply of postal telegraph forms, to enable passengers to originate postal telegram messages whenever the need arose. Any such postal telegrams handed to the travelling staff were taken to the telegraph office at the next stopping station, for transmission over the Company's lines to the central telegraph office where they were then passed over to the Post Office. Telegrams could be addressed to a named individual care of the station master at any LMS station as a courtesy service, but they had to be called for. This prompts the question of how would the recipient know that a message awaited him at the local station - obviously a forewarning to collect a message on a specified date would account for the bulk of such traffic.

A private telephone system was operated on the LMS network, not only linking stations with the area control room, but with direct extensions into major centres. Early in the life of the LMS, in September 1923, a new automatic telephone exchange with a capacity ultimately for up to 800 automatic lines each numbered on a three figure dialling system, was installed at Manchester (Victoria) Station. Links were made to the Post Office system to enable through calls to be made. More automatic systems were installed in later years.

The major part of the trunk telephone lines were between control offices, and in aggregate they were 4,600 miles long. Through this trunk communication, the Chief General Superintendent maintained a system of traffic control which had originated in 1906 with the Midland Railway Company.

Between the principal centres on the telephone system, these being St. Pancras and Derby, Derby and Leeds, Euston and Crewe, Crewe and Derby, there were several lines, and one improvement introduced to increase line capacity was the addition of 'carrier wave' circuits. Wherever there were two lines between the same centres, a third and fourth circuit could be superimposed over the two original circuits without the need for additional wiring, hence the 'phantom line' description by which the system was known. The telegraph and telephone sections came under the Chief Electrical Engineer's Department for maintenance purposes.

Plate 165   The telegraph office at Derby, pictured in 1930. The various baskets are labelled for Euston, Crewe and Post Office (No. 2), whilst the young female staff take an immobile position for the duration of this time exposure. The two fellows on the left of the picture thought they knew better - they were curious and moved. This scene is rather typical of the subdued office environment which was so prevalent in past years, a far cry from the less-regimented atmosphere found in most offices in this day and age. The telegraphists are facing machines which were the forerunners of today's Telex machines.

G. Waite

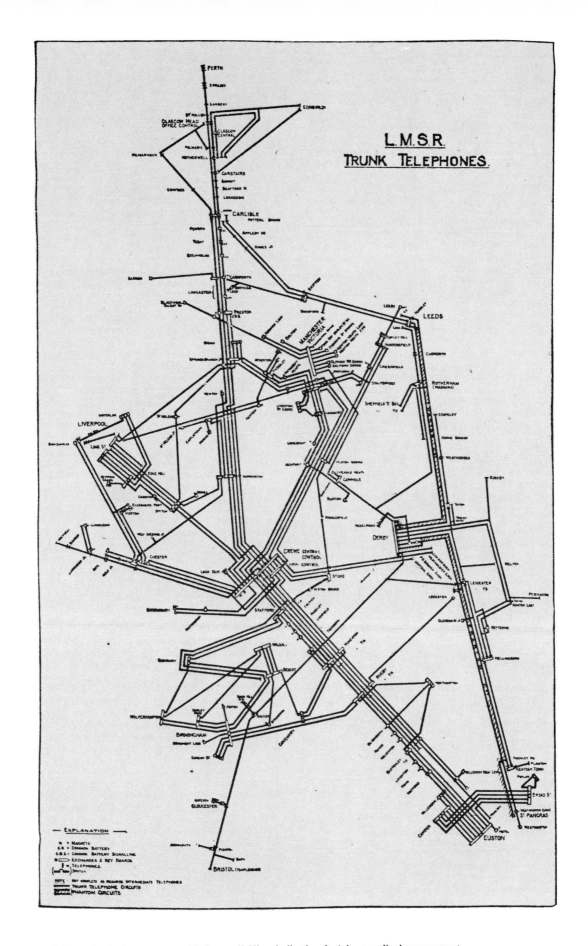

Plate 166   A diagram of the trunk telephone system, with the parallel lines indicating the 'phantom line' arrangement.

The Permanent Way

The railways of the present day owe their existence to, and are the practical result of the development of the ancient 'stone roads', 'wooden ways', 'plate ways' and 'rail-ways'.

In order to enable heavy loads to be conveyed with a minimum of hauling power, very early in history the wheel had been evolved as a means of moving objects.

The first 'stone road' consisted of two continuous lines of stones, each block being from 2ft. to 6ft. in length, 1ft. in width and about 6in. in thickness. The distance between the two lines of stones was 4ft., the outside width 6ft., with the wheel gauge 5ft. outside.

The first 'wooden way' is recorded as having been introduced for the conveyance of coal, from collieries to the docks in the Newcastle upon Tyne area. It consisted of cross sleepers placed about 2ft. apart, with wooden planks some 6ft. in length and 4in. wide being nailed to the sleepers. This development was in the early 1600s, and improvements were introduced in 1700 when the thickness of the timber was doubled, to become known as 'double wooden way'. The outside width or gauge was 5ft., to permit ordinary coal carts of the period to run on the new track. Flat cast-iron plates 3ft. long and ½in. thick were introduced in 1738, and nailed down to the timber to become the 'plated way'.

Wheels running off the track became a problem, causing a great deal of nuisance value, so in 1750 an upright wooden ledge was added to the outside of the already 'plated way'.

The 'iron plated way' caused considerable wear to the wooden wheels running upon it, and in 1753 the first cast-iron wheels were introduced. Wooden wheels running upon the 'wooden way' had caused few problems of wear, but the softer wood upon the iron plate was a different matter. An enterprising Mr James Outram, of Alfreton in Derbyshire, is credited with introducing the cast-iron wheel, and some 22 years later, he made a further innovation, no doubt as a result of the iron wheels causing considerable wear on the wooden ledge which had been added to the first 'plated way' in 1750.

Cast-iron plates 3ft. in length in the shape of a letter 'L' were cast, and two pieces were placed back to back upon the sleepers, with the upright section 4ft. 6in. apart. To install these plates, Mr Outram sent his own men, this giving rise to the term 'platelayer', which is still in use today. Iron wheels running upon this new iron track reduced wear, and for seventy years this new 'plate way' was known as 'Outram way'. The name 'tramway' soon evolved, when the first two letters of Mr Outram's name were omitted.

Stone returned to the scene when stone blocks were used on the Ticknall & Oakathorpe Tramway, to form the base for the 'L'-shaped cast-iron plates.

There followed a number of developments in the type and weight of the cast-iron plates used, until another engineer from the same area of Derbyshire, namely Butterley, a few miles south of Alfreton, designed an 'edge' rail system, known as the 'combination rail'. He was Mr William Jessop, and 'Jessop's edge rail-way' became shortened to the term 'rail-way', thus 'railway' has lived on.

Mr Jessop is also credited with having designed the wheel with the inside flange in 1789, and the fact that he decided first to have an outside gauge of 5ft., and then changed to an inside gauge without altering the rails, is said to be the reason why today we have a gauge of 4ft. 8½in., being 5ft., less the width of two Jessop rails.

The expression 'permanent way' described the road bed and superstructure of a finished railway, to draw the distinction from the contractor's 'temporary way', during the construction period.

The expressions 'tramway', 'railway' and 'permanent way' were all part of the scene when the London Midland & Scottish Railway came into being on 1st January 1923. These opening notes are merely to give the historical background to the terms which have been taken for granted by most people for well over 140 years.

Without these early pioneers, it could be argued that there would not have been a railway system at all, but this presupposes that only those whose names are recorded were capable of original thought. That was not the case, as there were others who made significant contributions, and not least of those was the man who first brought the steel rail to the railway.

It is recorded that the first steel rail was rolled by the Ebbw Vale Iron Company in 1857. It was known as Mushet's rail, after the engineer Robert M. Mushet, who had produced it from a Bessemer and Mushet ingot of steel. Prior to this time, the rails had been of iron.

The first length was supplied to the Midland Railway, who then installed it at Derby Station. Ten years later, in 1867, Mushet asked the Midland to resell the rail back to him, but in refusing, they promised him first refusal should they ever wish to dispose of this piece. Some six years later, however, Mushet again approached the Chief Engineer, a Mr J. S. Crossley, with a view to repurchasing the length, only to be told that it had been taken out of use and 'used up again'. Calculations were later made, to assess the wear it had been subjected to during the sixteen years it had been in use. On the basis that 250 trains, and at least 250 detached engines and tenders passed over it daily on 312 full working days each year, then around 1,252,000 trains and a similar number of light engine workings would have passed over it.

Two steel rails, each 21ft. in length, were laid at the Chalk Farm Bridge on the L&NWR on 2nd May 1862, side by side with two ordinary iron rails. Three years and three months later, the steel rails were taken up, after outliving sixteen ordinary iron rail faces, with the measured wear being only slightly more than one quarter of an inch. The result of this trial led the L&NWR to commence the changeover from iron to steel rails.

In 1923, the LMS adopted 60ft. steel bullhead rail, weighing 95 lb. per yard, and complying to British Standard Section. This followed a report of a committee of chief railway engineers, which had met to consider the types of rail previously used by the constituent companies. The Company exhibited a full 60ft. length of permanent way at the Wembley Exhibition, together with a section of rail, chair and fastenings to give the public a closer look. The 60ft. lengths of rail were supported on 24 creosoted Baltic redwood sleepers, with cast-iron chairs at the joints weighing 53 lb. each, and the intermediate chairs being 46 lb. each. The whole length was ballasted up with 1½in. granite ballast. Each chair was fastened to the sleepers by three 1in. galvanized steel chair screws, which passed through creosoted oak ferrules inserted in the chair screw holes, with a felt pad provided between the chair and the timber sleeper.

Completely new lines were now very rare, since the railway system had already reached the parts of the country which needed it. The new track, therefore, was required as a replacement for old and worn out stretches of constituent Company track, and a regular programme of re-laying was carried out to maintain the permanent way to a high standard.

Track mileage was generally divided into three main classes:

First - Main trunk passenger lines including passenger and important goods lines subject to regular express services and heavy traffic.

Second - Passenger lines, other than main trunk passenger lines, and goods lines subject to fast but not to heavy traffic.

Third - Virtually the remainder, meaning branch passenger lines over which traffic is light and speed is slow, or goods lines subject to slow or station to station traffic.

The main re-laying programme was concentrated on the first and then the second class lines, with an annual re-laying programme planned in relation to the measurable wear sustained by the various stretches of line. In deciding when a stretch of line required renewal, the engineer was influenced, and in fact still is, by the weight of the rails in use, and the annual loss per yard resulting from the extent of traffic using the stretch in question. Weighing machines or photographs of rail sections assisted the calculation of wear, but other factors were also taken into consideration. These included the depth of rail, whether the section was subject to brake power from trains, if on a facing falling gradient or on an incline, and whether the track section was curved, all were factors to be brought into the calculations.

With the programme of re-laying ready for implementation, gangs of about fifty men, including the ganger for the stretch of line to be re-layed and a timekeeper, were transported to the site. The speed with which the re-laying was completed, depended very much on the time the road could be broken between the necessary passage of trains. Short periods, of between ten and twenty minutes, were sufficient for a 60ft. length of rail to be taken out and replaced and the keys to be driven home, before the next train traversed the section very slowly. When sleepers as well as the rails were replaced, longer periods for the gangs to occupy the line were required and, consequently, this work was often undertaken at weekends when traffic was lighter and stretches of line could be closed. Points and crossings sustaining heavy wear often required replacement three or four times each year.

Sidings received little attention after being laid down, other than pointwork which was regularly greased and oiled.

The 'six foot' is the minimum permitted space between two sets of running lines, but in practice and on all curves, this distance was often greater than the minimum.

The annual consumption of permanent way materials was not inconsiderable. In an average year, between eighty and ninety thousand tons of steel rail and iron parts were used, along with well over one million sleepers and two million chairs and felt pads. The principal aim was to complete the annual renewal programme prior to the main holiday season, when traffic was greater and the Company wished to minimize delays through slow running.

With a gradual renewal programme to the new LMS standard, the Company was able to accelerate the services to give the passenger a better service. In 1933 for example, the Company claimed it had the greatest mileage, at 55m.p.h. or over, start to stop, of any line in Europe, with timetabled running of 7,898 train miles daily at this speed, compared with the next nearest company with 5,810 train miles.

The following photographs attempt to show some of the permanent way work carried out by the LMS, but in no way is this the complete array of what was achieved.

Plate 167 Tapton Junction, just north of Chesterfield, pictured just after a major re-laying programme in August 1931. The two lines to the right follow the path of the old North Midland Railway line to Rotherham, whilst the two on the left run on through Sheepbridge, Unstone and Dronfield to link up with the Hope Valley line at Dore & Totley. The long turn-out length allowed trains to pass over at normal speeds. There is much to interest the modeller in this picture, including the tidy ballasting and the trap points or switches, of which there are two types. The first is a single trap type, seen on the right-hand line, whilst the other is a point, positioned on the adjacent line. Whilst these protect the crossover from trains which may overrun signals at 'danger', close examination of this picture will reveal that rail brakes are mechanically linked to the switches. The rail brakes consist of lengths of machined rail fitted on the inside of the running rail. When the switch is set in the 'clear' road position, the rail brake is moved away from the running rail to give sufficient clearance for the wheels to pass. When the road is not 'clear', this rail brake fits closely up to the running rail, and should any train pass over this section of track, its wheels would be retarded through side pressure from the rail brake. If the driver was unaware of having passed a signal set at 'danger', then the crew would certainly be aware of the severe reduction in speed. The point and signal rodding from the signal cabin and signal wires and a host of other details may help the modeller in his search for detail.

G. Waite Collection

Plate 168 Permanent way men stand well clear of the running lines whilst this 'down' express train passes Brinklow, headed by No. 6142 *The York and Lancaster Regiment*. An engineering department train stands in the yard to the left of the goods shed, and a piece of rail in the 'six foot' suggests that these men are tidying up after some renewal work had been completed. From the signal cabin, the signal wires are carried on short posts until the sleepered barrow crossing is reached, then they are carried through into the foreground on low placed roller sets. The men may also have been clearing plant growth from the sleepered walkway to the barrow crossing.

G. Coltas

Plate 169 A painting by Stanhope Forbes, member of the Royal Academy, entitled 'The Permanent Way. Relaying'. This was one of a series of paintings commissioned by the LMS for poster use, to illustrate to the public some of the work carried out by the various departments of the railway which seldom came to the notice of passengers. This subject illustrates the labour-intensive re-laying work, and the back breaking job of lifting a rail, as any of those in the foreground would testify.

Author's Collection

Plate 170 Sandiacre in 1928, where a length of rail has just been manhandled on to the bolster wagon. Note there are three runners projecting at an angle from the wagon. The rail was lifted just above waist height where the three runners commenced, and was rested on the 'V' angle, before being pushed on to the bolsters.

G. Waite Collection

Plate 171 Extensive experiments were well under way in 1929 with steel sleepers as replacements for the traditional redwood timbers, and a number of types were tried at different locations. The LMS used the GKN steel trough type, with the chairs directly cast on to the steel pressing, with four heads to retain the chair formed on the underside, through metal passing through holes drilled in the sleeper. Small ballast gave the best rigidity, but the trough-shaped sleepers could still ride up the ballast within the trough. Replacement work is being carried out in this picture, and it is just possible to discern the mound of ballast left after the steel sleeper has been lifted away. The corners of the trough were pointed down to grip into the trackbed.

G. Waite Collection

Plate 172 In this picture, a section of steel-sleepered track has just been completed, with the discarded timber sleepers alongside. Comparison between the old and the new is possible in this view.

G. Waite Collection

Plate 173 With an increase in the number of high-speed trains causing extra wear on bullhead rail, experiments were carried out in 1936 with flat-bottomed rails, and here a section of track is shown under test at Cricklewood. Flat-bottom rail gave greater rigidity, weight for weight, than bullhead, and the first flat-bottom rail was of 110 lb. per yard, although later experiments were made using the 131 lb. per yard American standard rail. Again in 1940 and during the war years, further experiments led to flat-bottomed track becoming the standard to replace bullhead track, but this was one of the early decisions of the newly-formed British Railways, and a completely new rail section of 109 lb. per yard was to be used. Again, the LMS was one of the pioneers, of the flat-bottom rail in regular use.

National Railway Museum

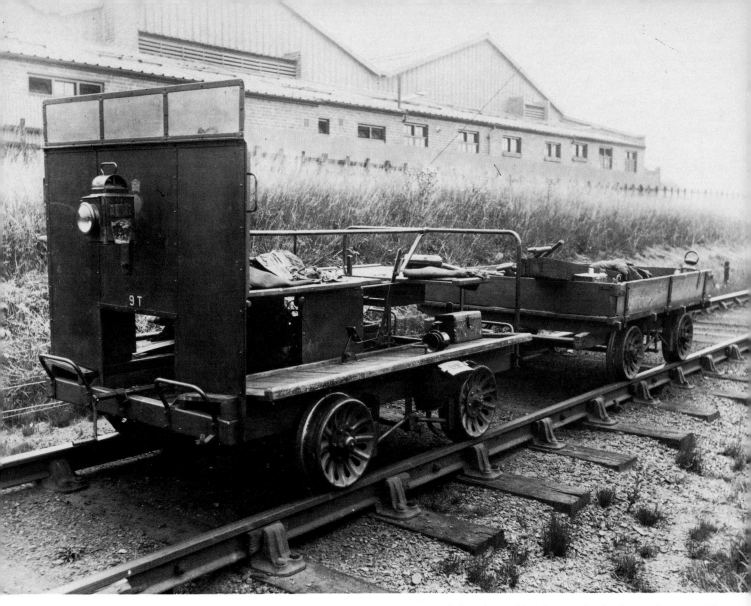

Plate 174 Day to day maintenance of the permanent way was carried out by length gangs, consisting of several lengthmen under the charge of a ganger. The principal duties of the gang involved the detection of any defects, whether on the track or other works, bridges, etc., and the repairing of any defect found under the direction of the ganger. Reports were required, and a systematic programme of maintenance was generally followed. Whilst most gangs of men walked the length allotted to them, those on branch lines were privileged, in that they were usually provided with a petrol driven trolley as a 'mobile gang', and were required to work over a longer stretch of line. This trolley and trailer is seen standing on the 'main' on the Swadlincote and Woodville loop of the Leicester to Burton Branch. The gang was responsible for the 7 mile 212 yd. length between Swadlincote Junction and Moira (Woodville Junction), plus the stretch from Woodville Goods Junction to the goods station at Woodville, or Wooden Box as it was first known, a distance of 1,584 yds. Motor trollies were usually signalled as a train, and they were treated as such when running through a section, with the train staff, tablet or token being carried on the trolley. A portable turntable and ramps were provided on each trolley, and the operation of removing the trolley from the track was a relatively quick and easy operation.

National Railway Museum

Plate 175 Whenever men were working on the line, a look-out was posted at either end of the group. His duty was to watch for signal movements and visible signs that trains were approaching, and to give a warning for the men to step away from the track and to ensure their safety. The men were identified by 'look-out' armbands, as shown in the picture. Footplate staff were, nevertheless, aware of work being carried out on the line, since the nature and location of the permanent way work was included in the notices published for the footplate staff.

Author's Collection

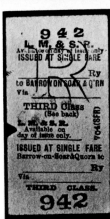

Plate 176 The Midland line to St. Pancras, pictured at Barrow-on-Soar in June 1926. Major bridge repair work is being carried out on the bridge which carries the railway over the River Soar, but of greater interest is the temporary realignment of the running tracks. Two tracks have been broken and slewed over, and the track has been temporarily interlaced around the work area. Close examination will show that this method avoids the need to lay-in points, and the slow moving trains merely traversed the additional running lines. Interlacing was also used for the renewal of track in cuttings or similarly restricted areas on plain track.

G. Waite Collection

Plate 177 The other end of the same site, showing the lines returning to the former trackbed. Switches requiring linkage to a lever frame were not required, but nose blocks were put in as though points were to be fitted. Both this and the previous photograph show a most interesting operation in progress. The two sections of severed track, seen on the right, have also been interlaced, to permit bridge reconstruction work.

G. Waite Collection

Chief Engineer's Department

This department, later to become the Chief Civil Engineer's Department, was responsible for maintaining no fewer than 28,000 bridges of all shapes and sizes, and on top of this figure, countless culverts. Some 10,500 of these were overbridges, and practically every known type of construction was to be found, be it of stone, brick, cast-iron or steel. Maintenance was continually carried out, and strengthening of earlier structures was often necessary to enable higher axleloads to be carried. The Chief Engineer's drawing office was located at St. Pancras, and a team of seventy draughtsmen and assistants were engaged in continually preparing drawings and specifications for new and replacement bridge works.

Repair and replacement work could, in many cases, be undertaken only between limited times and outside peak times, particularly where weekday traffic density was high on the main lines and suburban routes. In such cases, much of the work would be carried out during the hours of darkness or at weekends, when diversions to the less frequent Sunday services would be put into operation. When bridge replacement, rather than repair, was required, replacement steel bridge sections were assembled on a supporting structure alongside the old bridge. When ready, the old bridge would be demolished, and the new structure rolled into position. Often, within a short period of time, traffic could commence using the replacement bridge at very low speeds.

In 1937, there were 22 districts, each under the supervision of a District Engineer, with responsibilities for routine maintenance and annual inspection of all bridges in each district. The districts each had a staff which included bricklayers, joiners, plumbers, painters and other craftsmen, and any work found to be necessary could be carried out in a relatively short time.

In addition to the routine inspections, the linesman, who walked the section of the track daily, was responsible for reporting any matters relating to structures to the District Engineer.

Manchester District also had a specialist gang for bridge erection or steelwork repairs, who were available for work anywhere on the system.

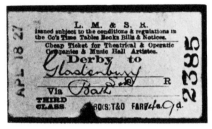

Plate 178 A major bridge replacement at Moira, on the Leicester to Burton branch line. The original bridge structure is still in place, but the brickwork has buckled through mining subsidence. The steel sections stand on rollers, ready for sliding into position.

G. Waite Collection

Plate 179 (above)   The same structure as seen in the previous photograph, viewed from track level on 17th June 1927. The workmen's train is on hand.

G. Waite Collection

Plate 180 (right upper)   A somewhat unusual bridge structure at Wincobank on the outskirts of Sheffield, in place to carry an overhead cable trolley system across the railway tracks, seen soon after completion in 1925. In addition to road and foot bridges, other bridge structures carried canals, water and other types of pipes across railway property. In all cases where special structures were provided for other than roadway or pedestrians, a wayleave or rental would be claimed by the railway company.

G. Waite Collection

Plate 181 (right lower)   A major reconstruction and repair job was necessary in 1932 for the 660ft. twelve arch viaduct across the River Trent, just a short distance to the south of Trent Junction. The original viaduct on this route had been built by the Midland Counties Railway in 1839, and when larger locomotives had entered traffic around the turn of the century, the Midland Railway had reconstructed the three steel girder sections in 1902, each 100ft. in length. In early 1932, the brick arches were found to have perished, and could no longer be relied upon without major attention. The piers, upon which the brick arch superstructure was built were not the problem, so these remained. The pillars were raised, and 168 steel girders, each 29ft. in length were placed upon them beneath the track but above the brick arches. The depth of filling between ballast level and the bricks was sufficient to allow the girders to be put in position. The programme commenced on 10th April, and was completed when speed restrictions were lifted on 7th June 1932. During this period, the line had been closed only on Sundays, when a 36 ton breakdown train had occupied the line. In this picture, the old brick viaduct, in the foreground, shows little sign of trouble, but to the left, four arches are already receiving attention, with the new steel girders resting on newly-raised pillars. This area of land has always been a flood area, and the water level here is 8 to 10ft. above normal, although it is suspected that someone has done a little artwork on the print to make it appear fast flowing. From the brake van, which is a late Midland or early LMS example, the remaining vehicles are, an Enderby & Stony Stanton Co. Ltd. five plank open, an ex-Caledonian four plank dropside, No. 340720, an unidentified sheeted wagon, 152838 LMS D1667 five plank open, 210592 a 10 ton ex-L&NWR five plank, 254166 LMS D1666 five plank open, an ex-CR four plank side door, possibly 307405, a fitted van No. 235857 and, on the right, an all-steel ventilated van, the number unfortunately being illegible.

G. Waite Collection

Plate 182   Steelwork for the viaduct reconstruction was supplied by Tyldesleys of Darlaston. The metal was received at the Trent sidings as individual 29ft. long girders, whereupon they were then assembled into groups of three, and encased in concrete and asphalt prior to being placed in position on the viaduct. In this view, the trainload in the foreground is ready for use, whilst the steelwork on the rearmost train is as received from the supplier.

G. Waite Collection

Plate 183   This view shows how the steel girders were placed on the newly-raised pillars, beneath the ballast level but above the brick arches. This was a major reconstruction job, which was completed with a great degree of ingenuity.

G. Waite Collection

Plate 186 The Civil Engineer's Department w. also responsible for tunnel work, and there we a number of old tunnels opened out to allow trac widening schemes to proceed. An example w. Cofton Tunnel, situated between Longbridge an Barnt Green, on the main line between Birmingha and Bristol, which was uncovered in 1926. Mo than 500,000 tons of earth and rock were remove from around the tunnel bore before the brick arc was demolished, and trains continued to pa through the tunnel throughout the eighteen mont period it took to excavate. In this view, th earthwork is nearing completion, and holes in th brickwork have been made which is temporari shored up to prevent collapse. The brick arch ha also been sectioned, so that final demolition an clearance can be done in stages. A large area of lan was involved, since the cutting was 80ft. deep an the sides had to be landscaped and shored to preve movement. This work was part of the quadruplir of track to provide greater traffic capacity on th stretch of line.

G. Waite Collectio

Plate 187 A remarkable view of the inside of Cofton Tunnel, just prior to demolition. Timber has been laid through the length of the tunnel to protect the trackbed and aid the removal of debris, once the supporting timbers have been removed and the crown dropped.

G. Waite Collection

Steam Turbine Locomotives

Various ideas for improving the efficiency of the conventional steam locomotive had been put forward by locomotive engineers over a long period of time, and well before the LMS period began. As a result, a number of experiments were carried out, all quite unsuccessful, so the quest for a new and more fuel efficient design went on, and just prior to the 1923 Grouping, the Ramsey Locomotive Company had built the Ramsey-Armstrong Whitworth turbine-electric condensing locomotive. It was tried out on the former L&YR metals in 1922, after permission had been given by the L&NWR, but it failed to perform successfully, despite numerous modifications, and was cut up in 1924.

From then on, attention was turned towards Sweden where the Ljungstrom Company had been undertaking experimental work, and the Directors of Beyer Peacock & Company authorized their Chief Engineer to collaborate with the Swedish company. As a result, a locomotive was designed and built by Beyer Peacock using the Ljungstrom technique under licence, and it ran for the first time on Sunday, 4th July 1926, over L&NER metals between Gorton and Woodhead. Some two months later, it was taken down to Derby to begin trials by courtesy of the L&MSR Board, whose interest in this new venture led to the offer of trials. At first it was confined to slow and semi-fast passenger trains between Derby and Manchester (Central) and it later returned to the Beyer Peacock Works for examination. Upon its return to Derby in March 1927, it then commenced work on passenger trains to Birmingham for a few weeks, and was then returned to work again to Manchester. Modifications were carried out when necessary, but its performance fell short of the design expectations, largely because of the limitations in size imposed by the loading gauge requirements in the British Isles. On the Manchester trips, speeds of 75m.p.h. were attained, but even greater speeds of up to 85m.p.h. were achieved when the engine was put to work on the heavier trains to St. Pancras in May 1927. Trials were later carried out with the Ljungstrom engine being measured against one of the Horwich 'Crabs' using a dynamometer car, and the most remarkable statistic to emerge from the trials was that the Ljungstrom engine used 84 per cent less water than the conventional 'Crabs'.

The locomotive was not unlike the 'Garratt' type which appeared later, but as can be seen from the accompanying photographs, it was a most grotesque-looking engine. It cost £37,000 to manufacture, against the average locomotive cost of £6,000, and a great deal of additional funding was required to enable the tests to be carried out and the design to be fully evaluated. The smokebox was some 6ft. in diameter and was 7ft. long; the driving wheels were 5ft. 3in. in diameter, the boiler barrel was 9ft. 6in. long and in entirety the weight was 143½ tons. The steam condenser was 4ft. 6in. in diameter and 27ft. in length with a condenser surface of 13,200 sq. ft. Water capacity was 2,550 gallons, and the coal capacity was 6 tons.

The Ljungstrom engine was returned to Horwich after comparative trials with the 2-6-0, and it remained intact until the early 1950s. The Beyer Peacock Company had hoped that interest would be aroused at a later date with the engine being put back into traffic, but it was a costly failure in comparative terms.

The third turbine locomotive to feature during the LMS period was, of course, No. 6202, a non-condensing turbine engine, built in 1935 in the Company's own workshops, which was known by the design name 'Turbomotive' rather than in the more traditional engine name manner. It was never officially named, but one wonders why it was never given a plate with the title 'Turbomotive' on it - the most obvious answer is where would it have carried it - on the nearside?

'Turbomotive' was by far the most successful of the turbine experiments, and whereas the earlier designs had been evolved as specially built one-off types, No. 6202 bore a great resemblance to the two Stanier 'Princess Royal' class Pacifics already in service, with the wheelbase and general appearance being almost identical. It was, at the outset, designed for express passenger service, and perhaps the most important aspect, of what was a new concept in locomotive propulsion, was its simplicity and straightforward design. Whilst the conventional steam locomotive was relatively easily constructed and maintained, and mechanical reliability was unsurpassed, there were disadvantages in the output of power which resulted in a 'hammerblow' effect at points on each revolution of the driving wheel. The 'hammerblow' effect produced uneven wear on both mechanical parts and on the track, and the aim with steam turbine locomotive designs was to eliminate this feature. It is a measured fact that the 'hammerblow' effect on a four cylinder engine was much less than on a two cylinder locomotive, but there was a limit to the number of cylinders which could be accommodated within the British

outline. With a steam turbine, there was no 'hammerblow' effect, and the whole motion could be balanced completely. The turbines for No. 6202 were manufactured at the Trafford Park Works of Metropolitan-Vickers Electrical Company Ltd., in Manchester, and were mounted on the locomotive frames which were sent specially from Crewe.

'Turbomotive' went into traffic in June 1935 and, although it spent some lengthy periods in the workshops, it completed 458,772 miles before being withdrawn and later rebuilt by British Railways in 1952. A regular working out of Euston with the 10.40a.m. 'down' service to Liverpool and the return working from Liverpool (Lime Street) at 5.25p.m. was the early scene for this engine, and some notable performances were recorded. The start-to-stop, between Crewe and Willesden Junction, was timed for an average speed of 64.5m.p.h., but speed was often higher than this, reaching, in some places, up to 90m.p.h. It was a quiet engine with a smooth exhaust, quite unlike the traditional thrust of a normal steam engine. It was a capable engine, and although modifications had to be carried out, it did show itself capable of meeting all requirements. The engine rode well and was noticeably smoother than a reciprocating engine and was very easy to control.

The main motive power unit comprised a multi-stage turbine and treble reduction gear, with the main forward turbine mounted on the nearside, with a smaller reverse turbine positioned on the offside alongside the smokebox. Steam from the boiler went to a steam-chest with six control valves which were operated from the cab. The regulator remained open whilst the engine was in steam, whether moving or stationary, and the power was gained through opening the six control valves progressively. The forward turbine was permanently coupled to the transmission gear, and to engage the reverse turbine and so enable the engine to move backwards, the engine had first to stop. A dog clutch was operated to engage the smaller reverse turbine, and as the engine moved back, the forward turbine was slowly rotated in the reverse direction, but without steam being on.

The average annual mileage of 'Turbomotive' over the first 8¾ years was 28,500 miles, but this period included some lengthy spells out of action. The comparable mileages for the 'Princess Royal' class engines was 53,000, and for the 'Coronation' class locomotives was 73,000 miles. The best years of its life were between 1936 and 1938, when it averaged 54,205 miles per year. Between 21st September 1939 and 24th July 1941, 'Turbomotive' was stored at Crewe, out of action due to the war conditions which prevailed at that time, and due to the demand for heavy express passenger engines, it was returned to traffic on this latter date.

'Turbomotive' could also lay claim to being the first engine in this country to be fitted with roller bearings for all axle journals of the engine and tender when built. It passed from LMS ownership in the 1946 lined black livery and with the addition of smoke deflectors. It was by far the most successful of the three types tested on LMS metals.

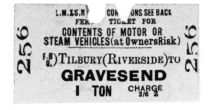

Plate 188   A rear view of the Ljungstrom engine. It was fitted with outside engine type plated frames, upon which was a 27ft. 9in. long by 4ft. 6in. diameter condenser, and the dished cover, on the front of what would normally be seen as the tender, was one end of the condenser. When operating, the condenser cylinder would normally be half full of water, around 1,350 gallons, and this provided the main supply for the boiler. Behind a totally enclosed cab, with its own but not uncommon problems in hot weather, was a coal bunker and between this and the condenser, the main turbine and gearbox, both made by the Ljungstrom Company in Sweden, and shipped to the United Kingdom. This picture was taken at Chinley on 15th December 1926, on one of the test runs.

S. T. Cowan/National Railway Museum

Plate 189   An 'up' express pictured at Derby, headed by the Ljungstrom engine. The louvred cold air intake to the smoke-box is shown in the open position.

D. Tee Collection

Plate 190 A close up view of the rear section of the Ljungstrom engine, showing the equalizing bars to the outside springing both above and below the footplate level, with part of the turbine and gearbox machinery in the somewhat cramped space between the coal bunker and condenser section.

S. T. Cowan/National Railway Museum Collection

Plate 191 The Ljungstrom 'Turbomotive' stands inactive alongside Derby Shed, and a good view of the shape of this rather ungainly machine is given. The massive size of the boiler can be seen, and at 6ft. diameter, it was the forerunner in size of the 'Garratt' boilers. The water tanks, seen alongside the boiler, carried 600 gallons. The front unit was, in fact, not powered, the turbine drive being connected to the coupled wheels beneath what appears to be the tender. Behind the five plank wagon, a 'Crab' 2-6-0 locomotive can be seen, possibly the one used in the tests referred to earlier.

N. Fields

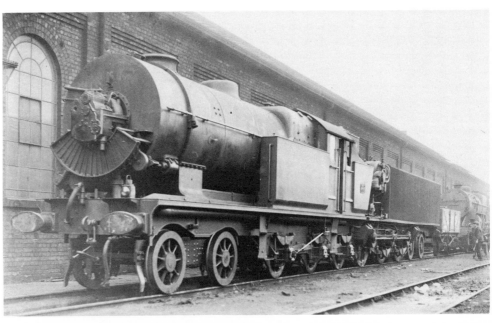

Plate 192 Again in traffic at Chinley, on 15th December 1926, the Ljungstrom engine awaits the home signal. The gentleman attending the front carriage is the ticket collector, an interested onlooker for the cameraman. The nearside of the engine was quite disappointingly plain above the footplate, but the offside carried a number of pipes and other items.

S. T. Cowan/National Railway Museum Collection

Plate 193 The Ramsey-Armstrong Whitworth engine, seen at Southport (Chapel Street) whilst on one of its forays from Horwich, pictured taking water for the return journey. Its massive proportions dwarf the coaching stock nearby, and there are a fair number of observers on the platform, to the left of the engine.

L&YR Society

Plate 194 Another photograph of the aforementioned engine; this time an oblique offside front view taken from the trackside.

L&YR Society

Plate 195 No. 6202 'Turbomotive' when new. The broad resemblance to the 'Princess Royal' class engines, Nos. 6200 and 6201 is evident in this view, and although the background is screened out, the picture was taken in Crewe Works yard.

National Railway Museum

Plate 196 The same engine, No. 6202, in service at Shrewsbury awaiting its turn to Crewe, a through working from the south-west. The smaller reverse turbine is encased at the side of the smokebox, and close examination will show the ventilation louvres which were added to the top edges of both turbine casings in the early months of 1936. These louvres were found to be necessary to assist in cooling the bearings, and to provide a free escape for any steam which passed the steam glands. Without free passage to the atmosphere, contamination of the oil by condensed steam would have been considerably increased. The engine is now fitted with its second boiler, with separate dome and top feed.

A. G. Ellis

Plate 197 No. 6202 in its final LMS guise; the 1946 livery. The larger reverse turbine casing is now fitted, together with a taller chimney. The smoke deflectors or 'wind-plates' were fitted when it left Crewe Works on 5th July 1939, and two and a half months later, in September 1939 at the commencement of World War II, it was withdrawn from traffic and placed in store, subsequently to re-emerge in 1941. The large 'keyhole', on the reverse turbine casing, allowed access to the leading sandbox filler. With the modern technology of today, not only in mechanical matters but also with advances in specialist oils, could 'Turbomotive' technology have been enhanced and the engine hugely successful?

Real Photographs

Basket Works

Butter making and duck rearing were the principal industries in the Aylesbury district when a basket making works was set up in 1876 and, four years later, the London & North Western Railway Company took the business over. Much of this traffic was despatched all over the country, and it is perhaps not surprising that the L&NWR, in an expansive period, quickly bought up this specialist business. In the early years of railway ownership, not only did the railway make the baskets, but they also packed the goods, particularly butter, prior to despatch.

Anyone who has noticed, in past years perhaps more so than in the last few years, the sturdy appearance of the baskets in general use on station platforms, as baskets or basket trolleys with wheels, may not be aware that the raw material for basketwork - osier rods - was grown in quantity in special plantations along a number of railway lines. Locations which had the right conditions for the plant were selected, and the resultant raw material did not cost the railway company anything other than the cost of harvesting the rods during winter time.

A number of skills were required to complete the basket, and not least amongst these was the finishing. A hide binding around the top edge, straps, buckles and identification plates were fitted, and on the larger baskets, wood slats were bolted to either the inside or outside, or on both sides and ends, greatly dependent upon the type of work the basket was to be used for. The L&NWR fitted enamelled identification plates to either side of the basket, signifying 'The property of . . .', but the LMS spray-painted the sides, ends and top when fitted, with large black letters 'L M S', and a reference number.

Several thousand baskets were owned by the LMS, and a large number lasted for many years. Repairs were also carried out at Aylesbury, but the relatively low cost of producing new baskets meant that any requiring substantial repair were merely written off.

Whilst the Aylesbury Works provided the LMS with most of its requirements, there were large numbers of other baskets to be seen on the railway at all times. The most obvious of these were, of course, the pigeon baskets. Such was the appeal of pigeons as a hobby and pigeon racing as a sport, that it would indeed be surprising if there was even one station on the LMS which had not, at some time, had even one pigeon basket consigned to or from it.

There was also a vast array in size and type of basket which were privately owned and which were consigned by rail, and this brought much needed revenue to the Company.

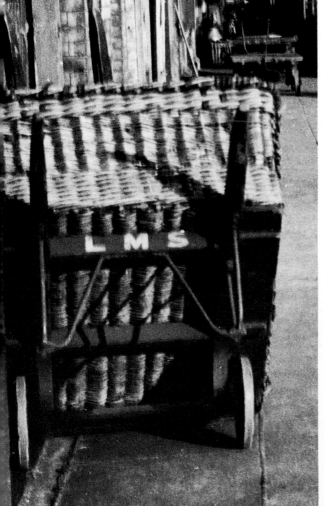

Plate 198 This photograph has been included to show the general style of a basket trolley built at Aylesbury, and which was primarily intended for station use. Whilst the metal plate indicates L&NWR ownership, many of the trolleys and basket barrows remained in service right through the LMS period, in some cases the baskets never being lettered LMS.

Author's Collection

Plate 199 A former L&NWR two-wheeled basket barrow, with the addition of LMS lettering on the frame.

G. Coltas

Plate 200 Pigeons in baskets stacked on the platform always drew the attention of passengers, if only out of curiosity to see where the birds were destined, or had come from, to be released. Empty baskets had to be returned to sender and, in all respects, it was a two-way business. The season generally extended from April to September, and whilst some journeys for the younger birds were relatively short, others travelled to more far-flung parts of the country. In an average season, more than two million pigeons were transported by LMS trains, and for the major races, special trains of vans were run. These included around twenty vehicles, all heated and illuminated throughout the journey, and accompanied by pigeon club officials as attendants. The 1928 season saw a peak with over seven million pigeons carried, with as many as seventeen special trains being run on peak days. Prior to each season, the LMS issued a pigeon train service programme, running to some 80 pages, setting out the race programme and a matching van service, and details of the various homing clubs. Station staff were regularly called upon to release birds and mark the time of release on the basket label, and then return the basket on the next homeward bound train, for which the charge was 4d each. The full charge for the outward journey varied between 1s 2d and 2s 6d. For the LMS Fur and Feather Society, which had many pigeon fanciers as members, specially reduced rates for conveyance of birds were agreed. In this photograph, a full brake van is being loaded from a former L&YR platform trolley, 'somewhere on the Central Division'.

Author's Collection

Plate 201 A scene so typical of the railway goods yards in the 1920s and 1930s, and a considerable number of empty baskets in this view of Oldham's Werneth yard in 1932, no doubt having been returned for reuse in the town's then thriving cotton industry. This type of tapered basket was often known as a 'skip', and to the right of centre, a number of lids are stacked together. There are a number of other features in this picture which may be of interest to the railway modeller. Note the loaded wagon in the foreground, a variety of empties and the large area of sleepered platform, with the edge sleepers following the track contour on the curve. The man to the left of the picture is leaning on packing cases labelled 'A. Stott & Sons Ltd. Oldham', and if my memory serves me correctly, this company manufactured fish-frying equipment. If the private owner wagons are to be believed, much of the coal traffic came from the South Yorkshire, Derbyshire and Nottinghamshire areas. For those modelling a goods yard, this view gives a good idea of what is required to achieve a measure of realism.

V. R. Anderson Collection

Registered Transit of Freight

In 1933, the 'Big Four' railway companies introduced a scheme for expediting the transit of merchandise and livestock by goods train under the 'Green Arrow' banner. For a special fee of 2s 6d per consignment in addition to the normal freight rates, whether it was a single package or a whole train load, the consignment was kept under special observation from the time it was entrusted to the Company to the time of delivery, and it was sent by the most rapid goods train transit possible. Whilst this must have been something of an innovation for merchandise, it is perhaps surprising that livestock was included in the 'Green Arrow' service. With the feeding and watering of livestock during the journey, quite often accompanied by a drover, it was in the interest of the Company to move them as speedily as possible, to avoid unnecessary stress and fatigue for the animals, as they weren't interested in long journeys and red engines!

Every effort was made to advise the recipients that packages had arrived for them, and for those who wished to know in advance, the Company would ascertain details by telegraphic advice from the despatching station. This would specify when and by which route the package had been sent forward, and the expected time of arrival. If the sender so wished, he too could be advised when delivery had been completed.

In order that consignments sent under these arrangements could be readily identified, a green paper arrow was gummed to the address labels on the packages, and attached to the consignment note, invoice and wagon labels, and an example of this is shown in *Plate 202*. The service was a success, and on 1st January 1936 a further registered service was introduced for transit by passenger train, and this carried the title 'Blue Arrow'. The same 'Green Arrow' standards of service applied to the new 'Blue Arrow' service, but journey times by passenger train were lessened.

The Railway 'C O D' (Cash on Delivery) service was introduced experimentally from 1st July 1934, for an initial period of twelve months. In the first month, 1,261 consignments were dealt with but within a few months, the monthly 'C O D' figures had risen to around eight thousand, and were increasing. At first, the value of consignments was not allowed to exceed £40, but this figure was later increased to £100 and charges were by way of a commission fee based on value with a minimum of 6d and a maximum of 5s 0d.

The three services previously discussed were very successful, and brought much needed traffic to the railways in a period when competition from road-throughout carriers was increasing.

Plate 202   To distinguish them from standard rate items, and on the relative paperwork, the same design and size of arrow, in green and blue respectively, was used. ERO 29825 was the 'green' stock code.

Author's Collection

Freight Traffic

Plate 203 Evesham is a place name synonymous with fresh fruit and vegetable growing, and in order to move the produce to the housewives in all parts of the country, special trains left the town each day to ensure wagons reached their destinations no later than 7.00 the following morning. London traffic arrived at the wholesale markets in the city in the early hours. Between five hundred and one thousand wagons a week were sent into Evesham to be loaded and consigned away and, in this view, a specially-posed publicity picture, the train is about to leave for the north.

Author's Collection

Plate 204 Two stickers which need little explanation. They were affixed to cartons, packages and invoices, in order to attract more traffic. They are maroon and white, with the larger one having black shading to the lettering.

Author's Collection

Plate 205 A sheeted wagon, pictured with the lettering nicely placed. The wagon is a one plank type, with the tarpaulin just failing to cover the LNWR lettering on the wagon side. The figures 11/26 indicated November 1926, the date when the sheet was last waterproofed. The presence of the two men would suggest this was a wagon specially sheeted to show how a tall load on a low wagon should be treated. Neither man has the cap badge, and one has a button in his pocket ready for the wife! The horse vehicle to the left is No. 9433, a type 45 in the first livery style, with either grey or Post Office Red wheels. The ex-L&NWR van with roof door on the right has received its new LMS numberplate of 264232. The L&NWR numberplate appears to have been removed, and the screws replaced.

Author's Collection

Plate 206 Earlestown Station in winter, with a specially-posed open carriage truck, No. 4792, pictured when carrying six small open fish containers. These were part of one lot of eighteen PF class containers built at Earlestown in 1936, and lettered for Fleetwood to Belfast, via Heysham, fish traffic. The sides and ends folded down flat, to save space when being returned empty.

V. R. Anderson Collection

Plate 207 Derby St. Mary's Goods Yard, featuring a long low wagon loaded with pipes, en route from Leicester to Bridgewater Junction on 16th August 1937. This was a photograph taken to illustrate an example of a badly loaded wagon. The pillars on the loaded bolster wagon to the left have been moved up to the load on the end bolsters, to prevent side movement. On the right, an ex-Midland three plank dropside wagon, No. 29519, is carrying a German Railways wooden container, and there are a number of other goods wagons, including a line of seven private owner and GWR and LNER examples.

Author's Collection

Plate 208 Tamworth Co-operative Society horse-drawn bread delivery vans arriving new from the body builders. They were very similar to the final LMS standard type of horse-drawn van, type ST100, but unlike the LMS vans, these had mud-guards embellishing the rear wheels, which were steel pressings fitted with internal drum brakes and pneumatic tyres. The wagon to the right is No. 345357, an ex-Caledonian vehicle fitted with LMS axleboxes, whilst the three other vehicles are ex-Midland stock.

Author's Collection

Plate 209 Instruction books on the loading of specific types of traffic were provided at all goods stations, and round rigid timber was one such commodity. This self-contained load required a guard wagon, because the length of the tree trunk could not be contained within the length of the ex-MR bogie bolster wagon. More than 60,000 tons of round timber was regularly carried by the Company each year, with total loads in some years exceeding 100,000 tons. Bowler hats and homburgs would suggest that a posse of local railway managers have witnessed the loading of this enormous chunk of timber.

Author's Collection

Plate 210   Approximately one million pigs a year were carried by the LMS, and close on fifty per cent were consigned from LMS stations. This is a typical livestock market scene, with the railway staff waiting to load a double deck sheep or pig lorry.

British Railways

Plate 211   Sheep being chaperoned into cattle stalls at Rugby, on 6th February 1933, this being a dull wet day. More than two thirds of the total head of live-stock carried were sheep, with between six and seven million being consigned by the LMS each year, eighty per cent originating from LMS stations.

National Railway Museum

Plate 212 A cattle train pictured in July 1937 standing in Brinklow Station on the 'down' main line, with Compound No. 1156 blowing off. There were no cattle dock facilities at Brinklow, so the reason for the stop was not to put vehicles into the yard for loading or unloading. One and half million head of cattle was carried by the Company each year in the 1930s, and around 73 per cent of this originated from stations on the LMS system. In addition, cattle and other livestock was transported in Company road vehicles between sale markets and farms or abattoirs, without ever being carried on rail.

G. Colta

Plate 213 Former L&YR 0-6-0 locomotive No. 12243, pictured on the Sowerby Bridge troughs with a mixed freight train. The interesting thing is that the troughs were on a curve, and with the normal cant on curves to counteract the centrifugal force, the maximum amount of water would be less than in a level set of troughs of the same length. The trough itself would have to follow the line of the curve, and be canted to allow the tender scoop to keep its line in the trough.

G. Coltas

Plate 214 Ex-L&NWR Class 7F 0-8-0, No 9436, seen heading a coal train at Milverton, Warwickshire in 1946.

G. Colta

Plate 215   A former North London Railway 0-6-0T, photographed in the serene pastures of North Derbyshire on the Cromford & High Peak Railway, soon after nationalization. Both the engine and wagon still carry LMS lettering and British Railways numbering, but at least the wagon has had 'M' added to the LMS number. Just to the left of the board, prohibiting the engine from moving forward until clearance was given by the station master at Friden, is another engine, shunting at Friden.

V. R. Anderson

Insurance of Livestock

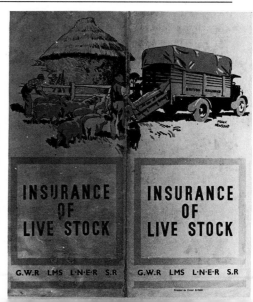

Livestock, carried by rail or rail company road vehicles, could be insured under a scheme arranged by the four rail companies against death or injury during transit. For the princely sum of 1d, a calf was insured for £2 maximum, while for 6d, a cow or bull was covered for up to £25 per head. Horses and ponies cost 8d per head for a value up to £50 and for 2d, a bacon pig was insured for up to £6 whilst a 'porker' pig still cost 2d for an insurance of £3.

The scheme did not cover imported animals railed from British ports, and there were certain exclusions to the cover as one would expect. Death by disease, death or injury due to the animal being pregnant or through the birth of young during transit, death or injury as a result of persons engaging in any railway strike, war action or any damage incurred through animals coming into contact with disinfectant used on the rail vehicles, were all exclusions.

Plate 216   The outer cover of the pamphlet giving details of the insurance available.

L. Knighton Collection

Dynamometer Car Running Tests on Locomotive Performance

These vehicles were marshalled immediately behind the tender, to allow measuring apparatus on the tender to be linked by cable directly to the car. An observer also travelled on the footplate, to take notes and record details, during the trip, on boiler pressure, regulator and reversing gear positions.

Instruments in the main area of the car recorded data on a slowly moving roll of calibrated paper, to give a permanent record of the trip. One interesting feature was that when the locomotive was pulling the train along, the line to indicate the drawbar pull was above the datum line, and when the brakes were applied, the drawbar line crossed to below the datum, indicating that the train was pushing the engine along.

A member of the dynamometer car staff was responsible for activating a pen which was used to mark the positions of stations, junctions and other features such as water-troughs on the paper record.

In Volume 1 of *LMS Miscellany, Plate 216* the ex-L&YR dynamometer car is seen behind the tender of 'Turbomotive', No. 6202 in May 1936, when tests were carried out with this engine on the 'Royal Scot' service between Euston and Glasgow (Central).

The object of dynamometer car tests was to ascertain the pull exerted by the engine, the speed of the train throughout the run and the amount of work done by the engine during the course of the tests. This somewhat simplistic statement covers a wide range of accurately measured data, which was necessary to enable different classes of locomotive to be assessed against one another, in as near identical conditions as practicable, and to further the research into the most efficient use of coal and water in locomotive boilers.

Plate 217a   The former Lancashire & Yorkshire Railway dynamometer car showing the raised panelling which provided a viewing gallery for the technical staff. No. 10874 is in the first LMS livery, and was later renumbered 45050 after 1933. The vehicle is carried on its original L&YR bogies, but later one of these was replaced by an LMS bogie.

National Railway Museum

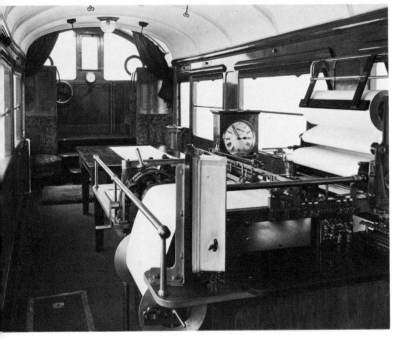

Plate 217b   The instrument room in the ex-L&YR car, showing the delicate measuring instruments mounted on a cast-iron table. At the far end of the car is a raised platform, which was always immediately behind the tender to give the staff a good view of the road ahead and the footplate.

National Railway Museum

Plate 218   The ex-Midland Railway Directors' Saloon, allocated No. 45052 in the dynamometer car series, seen here coupled to a 'Patriot' class engine, No. 5533 on 24th September 1934. The engine is fitted with a front shelter, and is wired up for a series of smokebox gas analysis tests.

F. W. Shuttleworth Collection

The LMS School of Transport

Plate 219   The LMS School of Transport was planned in 1936, with the stone-laying ceremony being performed by Sir Josiah Stamp on 22nd September 1937. The official opening, on 22nd July 1938, was performed by the then Minister of Transport, Rt. Hon. Leslie Burgin, MP. Located in Osmaston Park, Derby, a quarter of a mile from the Carriage & Wagon Works, the school facilities included residential accommodation, for up to fifty railway students. This view is one taken on completion of the building, but before the ground had been laid out with lawns and other landscaping.

Author's Collection

Plate 220   A most interesting feature in the dining room of the school is shown in this view. It is a wall mural depicting 100 years of transport, with all items shown in motion. On the right, the earlier forms of transport are seen, followed by more modern modes as one casts one's eye towards the left of the mural. Although this view does not show the full mural, it is nevertheless full of interesting details. One such item of interest is a horse-drawn open van, with a Brunswick Green canvas tilt. It confirms that the colour of the canvas in the late 1930s was green, and not exclusively black or grey. Long may this mural remain.

Photographed by John Edgington
Reproduced by kind permission of Charles Underhill, Principal of the Railway Engineering School, Derby

The Manchester School of Signalling

Plate 221   An interesting display for training signalmen. The '1' gauge model track was used to demonstrate the working of the railway, using the signal cabin block instruments assembled in front of the screen. The presence of the white screen was a temporary addition to the school, and it appears to be just a white linen covering, with the pictorial posters being added to brighten and widen the sphere of interest. In the bottom left corner, a table selection of timetables and booklets, together with the posts and chain, suggest the photograph was taken during preparations for a Directors' visit or an open day. The Signalling School was opened by the L&YR and is still in use today in the Manchester (Victoria) Station buildings. A similar block signalling layout was installed in the LMS School of Transport, Derby which was opened in 1938, but was removed some years ago.

National Railway Museum

Turntables

Turntables were to be found at most engine sheds and at some of the larger stations, and it was the locomotive crew's duty to turn the engine whenever this was necessary. The earliest tables were push operated, and providing the locomotive being turned was balanced on the table, so as to avoid more weight at one end than the other, two men could slowly turn the table to the position required.

Plate 222 Inverness Motive Power Depot, with a former Highland engine being turned. The two men are pushing with feet braced against the running rails, as there appears to be little else to use as a foothold. In later years, it was realized that this was a hazardous operation, so the edge surrounding the turntable well was levelled up, and bracing bars were fitted as shown in the following photograph.

G. Coltas

Plate 223 This photograph was taken for an accident prevention booklet, and shows the correct way of taking the strain to push the turntable round. The driver is able to take a good foothold against the bars, and with a level surface there is less likelihood of a foot slipping under the strain, and is therefore much safer. The bar protruding from the table, against which the driver is pushing, was retractable, but this gave good leverage.

British Railways

Plate 224 In all respects, this photograph gives the modeller a good deal of detailed information to enable an accurate model to be constructed. However, this 70ft. turntable at Derby was vacuum-operated from the engine, thus the hard work had been taken out of the turning operation. The 70ft. turntable at Euston was fitted in 1932, and was so finely balanced that despite its size and weight with a locomotive thereon, it could be turned by one man. In 1935, the Euston table became the first to be fitted with a vacuum engine, and as this was considered successful, other turntables were fitted with similar equipment. This view of Derby was taken on 27th August 1936, and the locomotive is one of the Vulcan Foundry 'Black Fives', with lettering on the tender more closely spaced than was normal.

V. R. Anderson Collection

Plate 225 This view of Polmadie Shed shows the location of the turntable in relation to the rest of the shed area, and the fact that it had only one road to and from it. It is a small push-operated table. Polmadie was the principal locomotive shed in the Glasgow area and, in the later years of 1944/5, had an allocation of twelve 'Coronation' class engines. The outbuildings, the two water tanks, the signal gantry, the shed building, the coal supply and barrel clutter all combine to make an interesting scene for the modeller.

British Railways

Plate 226 The erecting shop at St. Rollox Works, with a host of former Caledonian engines in evidence, in December 1925. No. 14750, one of the McIntosh 49 class 4-6-0 locomotives, was one of two forerunners of the 'Cardean' class, built by the Caledonian in 1903.

National Railway Museum

Under Repair

Plate 227 A Johnson Class 3P 4-4-0 locomotive, pictured whilst receiving attention at Derby Works in 1931. Some engines of this class lasted right through the LMS period, although the bogie brakes were later removed. Judging by the amount of stopper applied to the wheel splasher and cabside, as well as the firebox wrapper, it is suggested that corrosion had been one of the problems on this locomotive.

G. Coltas

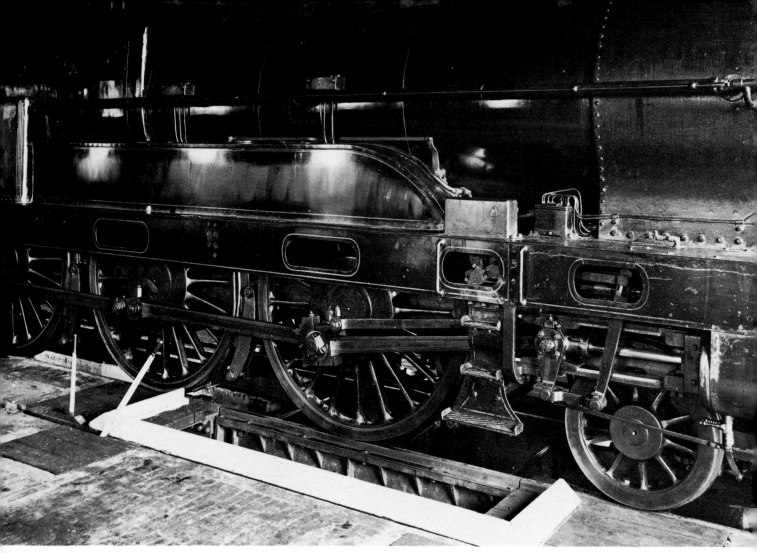

Plate 228   Bedford Motive Power Depot in August 1932, with an unnamed 'Claughton' class engine positioned over the wheel drop. This was a device which allowed individual axles to be removed from engines when they required attention, and enabled repairs to be carried out locally without the need to send engines to the works. There is much to interest the modeller in this picture, with some superb engine details in close up.

V. R. Anderson Collection

Plate 229   'Coronation' class, No. 6224 *Princess Alexandra*, newly outshopped in Crewe Works Yard on 23rd June 1946, after the removal of the streamlined casing. The tender has been painted, lined and lettered, and the high gloss finish is reflecting the bright light around. There are a number of features which should be of interest to the model railway enthusiast. The tender sides extend a short way beyond the end of the tender and, on the streamlined tenders, the rear edge of the side-sheets were extended, and a foot or so above the tender footplate level, they curved in to meet the rear edge of the footplate. This view shows that the side-sheets have been cut back, but not fully. The brackets are still in position, together with the step-ladder. A rear vertical handrail and footsteps were not necessary, and cut-outs have now been made in the frames.

W. L. Good

Internal Works Transport

All day and every day, a variety of small transport items was in use in the various workshops, to move the smaller items between points to keep the works going. Large items, such as locomotive boilers, carriage bodies, etc. were moved by overhead cranes, but the many types of castings, forgings and multitude of nondescript items were moved by handtrucks and petrol or battery-driven vehicles. These were small enough to be able to move between the machinery in the works, yet sufficiently powerful to move a collection of the small heavy items.

A large number of handtrucks were of the Company's own manufacture, with modifications to the standard platform trolleys and barrows, to enable them to be used for specialized work.

The following photographs do no more than illustrate a small number of types, and the many hundreds of others must, alas, remain anonymous.

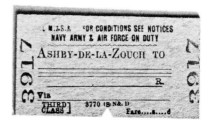

Plate 230 In 1934, an engineer by the name of F. E. Bagnall was asked by the LMS Railway to design and develop a small petrol-engined tractor for station platform work, with the resultant vehicle being designated an 'Imp' tractor. In addition to platform work, they were used in and around the railway workshops, and at the end of the World War II period, many were reconditioned for further use. Development continued, and the Model 'A' was introduced, with the LMS placing orders to add to its 'Imp' fleet. The new model was demonstrated to the Company at Crewe and in this picture, it is being driven by a Lansing Bagnall engineer, with a train of five trolleys specially-adapted for works use.

Lansing Bagnall

Plate 231 A Lodemor battery-electric truck, seen in the tarpaulin sheet works at Osborne St., Manchester. The truck is carrying a platform similar to the ones standing to the front and rear, and this principle was similar to the lift-off flats used with horse-drawn and motor vehicles. A later patented system was the 'Jak tug' system, using hand-operated trolleys. Special linen sheets were provided, to cover flats of cloth prior to being sheeted with oil-dressed tarpaulin sheets which, if they came into direct contact with the cloth, would cause irreparable damage. The whole of the special linen sheet stock was based at Salford Station, Manchester, under the control of the Salford goods agent, and overall supervision of the Manchester District Goods Manager. There were a number of sheet concentration depots to which surplus sheets and ropes were forwarded by the stations each day, and requirements for sheets were fulfilled by these depots.

British Railways

Engines and Carriages

There are specialist books available on locomotives, and the small selection of pictures which follows is a personal one. The bigger engines were well-known, and moreover remembered, particularly when someone could recount a 'record' time behind a Pacific or 'Royal Scot'. Nevertheless, the engines that seldom captured the spotlights were just as important in the railway scene.

Plate 232 An unidentified 'Royal Scot' class locomotive approaches Lichfield (Trent Valley) Station from the south, photographed through the L&NWR pattern signal post which stood adjacent to the road overbridge. The signals on the right governed the entrance to the 'down' slow line through the platform.

V. R. Anderson Collection

Plate 233 The station pilot, pictured at the south end of Sheffield (Midland) Station in the lazy days of summer. No. 1396 had been rebuilt sometime after 1925, and given a Belpaire firebox. The lattice bridge led from the roadway, in front of the railway cottages in the background, across the station area and to the roadway on the town side of the station.

A. G. Ellis

Plate 234 An 'action' picture, with No.1172, an LMS Compound, built in 1925, taking on water, and the ex-L&NWR carriage getting more than a fair wash. More than 9,000 million gallons of water were consumed by LMS engines, including the not inconsiderable quantities which were spilt at trough locations such as this.

W. L. Good per W. T. Stubbs

Plate 235 Just prior to the outbreak of war, on 25th May 1939, crimson and gold 'Coronation' class Pacific, No. 6228 *Duchess of Rutland* coasts along with a six coach express for Euston at Town Thorns, near Rugby. This was a rather splendid sight in the Northamptonshire countryside.

G. Coltas

Plate 236 Rebuilt 'Royal Scot', No. 6133 *The Green Howards* is pictured leaving Carlisle for the north. For enthusiasts living in the Midlands or on the west side of the country, this engine was one of the hardest to find, and I recall that a sighting at Leicester, on the 'Thames-Clyde Express' on one occasion, was 'the event of the year' in the 'spotting' world. It is shown with a 20A (Holbeck) shed plate and in the 1946 livery.

V. R. Anderson Collection

Plate 237 The halcyon days of 1925, and an 0-6-0 locomotive leans to the curve at the entrance to Headstone Tunnel, running light engine back to shed.

D. Ibbotson Collection

Plate 238 A three coach express! headed by Stanier Pacific, No. 6201 *Princess Elizabeth*, moves empty carriages through Crewe Station, the last one being a former L&YR electric carriage. Those who can remember the steam days at Crewe will recall the rather greasy area at the north end, shown here, where express engines stood to take on water.

B. C. Lane

Plate 239 Oh dear driver, how did you get the leading wheels on both carriages off the track? The location is on the Swadlincote loop line, off the main Leicester to Burton line. It is quite an intriguing incident, but how did it happen? There are several points to note; little damage to the track, other than a score line along the ends of the sleepers, and people on the bridge, but no one on the engine, in the train, or on the track admiring this amazing incident. Could it be a 'staged' affair with bags of realism? . . . I really don't know . . .

Author's Collection

Plate 240 Brinklow Station in 1938, with a Fowler 2-6-4T in the 'up' slow platform, on a Nuneaton to Rugby local passenger train.

G. Coltas

Plate 241 One of eight former North Staffordshire Railway 0-6-4 tank engines built in 1914/15 wartime conditions, pictured on home territory at Stoke-on-Trent in 1930, with a stopping train to Derby. There is much to interest both the modeller and historian in this view. The valancing is of NSR origin, the platform trolleys just ahead of the engine are both bought-in examples, and there is a rather splendid small bracket signal with two underslung metal dolls. Note, too, the spring-loaded catch point in the foreground.

G. Coltas

Plate 242 A Kirtley double-framed 0-4-4WT, No. 1208, seen on station pilot duties at St. Pancras in 1930, some sixty years after it first entered service with the Midland Railway. The engine is a most interesting example, yet is a type very rarely modelled. No. 1208 is pictured carrying shed plate No. 16 (Kentish Town). The lamp brackets are unusual, in that the centre one on the footplate is level with the footplate, and there is also one with a lamp on it above and in line with the brackets above the buffers. There is also duplication of the smokebox door bracket. This arrangement may well have been required, as some of these engines were fitted with condensing apparatus for working the tunnel route to Moorgate. The lamp-post is worthy of note as the base is a Midland casting, with the base section positioned above platform level. The shoulder section, which is just below the engine numberplate level, was normally sunk into the ground, and an extension piece has been inserted below the crossbar to give even greater height. The lamps with the extension piece were also used in goods yards and, in fact, some were still in use in the yard to the west of Nottingham (Midland) Station in 1982. On the far platform, a collection of platform barrows and trolleys, mostly types 200 and 201, can be seen, along with two water bowsers used for refilling toilet water tanks in carriages.

G. Coltas

Plate 243 Pictured in half-and-half livery is No. 46253 *City of St. Albans*, on 11th September 1949, almost exactly three years after first entering service as the first large engine built by the LMS after the war. The livery is the 1946 black with crimson footplate edging and straw lining, the only LMS livery this engine ever carried. A cast BR numberplate is awaited, but the cab-side carries the new number. This engine had the shortest life of any of the LMS 'Coronation' class locomotives, being withdrawn 16 years and 134 days after entering service. The BR-built *City of Salford* was the only one in service for a shorter period, 18 days less than *City of St. Albans*.

T. J. Edgington